THE HOLLYWOOD
HISTORICAL FILM

NEW APPROACHES TO FILM GENRE

Series Editor: Barry Keith Grant

New Approaches to Film Genre provides students and teachers with original, insightful, and entertaining overviews of major film genres. Each book in the series gives an historical appreciation of its topic, from its origins to the present day, and identifies and discusses the important films, directors, trends, and cycles. Authors articulate their own critical perspective, placing the genre's development in relevant social, historical, and cultural contexts. For students, scholars, and film buffs alike, these represent the most concise and illuminating texts on the study of film genre.

THE HOLLYWOOD HISTORICAL FILM

ROBERT BURGOYNE

BLACKWELL PUBLISHING
350 Main Street, Malden, MA 02148-5020, USA
9600 Garsington Road, Oxford OX4 2DQ, UK
550 Swanston Street, Carlton, Victoria 3053, Australia

First published 2008 by Blackwell Publishing Ltd

1   2008

Library of Congress Cataloging-in-Publication Data

Burgoyne, Robert, 1949–
   The Hollywood historical film / Robert Burgoyne.
      p. cm. — (New approaches to film genre)
   Includes bibliographical references and index.
   ISBN 978-1-4051-4602-9 (hardcover : alk. paper) — ISBN 978-1-4051-4603-6
(pbk. : alk. paper)   1. Historical films—United States—History and criticism.   I. Title.

   PN1995.9.H5B89 2008
   791.43′6580973—dc22

                                                            2007024732

A catalogue record for this title is available from the British Library.

Set in 11/13pt Bembo
by Graphicraft Limited, Hong Kong

For further information on
Blackwell Publishing, visit our website at
www.blackwellpublishing.com

This book is dedicated to my mother,
Patricia O'Donnell Burgoyne

CONTENTS

ILLUSTRATIONS

ACKNOWLEDGMENTS

I would like to begin by acknowledging Barry Keith Grant, the editor of the series in which this book appears, for his insight, diplomatic manner, and exceptionally good ear. Prompt, responsive, and always gentle with his advice, he has the gift of providing just the right touch and just the right amount of pressure to yield the best results. I would also like to thank Jayne Fargnoli from Blackwell, who has been a warm and encouraging editor throughout. Her approach to publishing makes this work a more personal project than it might otherwise have been: the times when I felt I should make an extra effort were almost entirely due to the sense of friendship I felt with her, and my desire not to disappoint. Thanks also to Ken Provencher for very skillful and professional help. For intellectual support, I must thank Robert Rosenstone, whose work I continue rely upon, not only for insights and ideas, but for the confidence to proceed. When doubts about the value of writing about history and film come knocking on the door, his work, and personal support, have served to drive them away. His determination to make the case, again and again, for film as a medium of historical thinking is a model of conviction and purpose. His pioneering work in this field will not be equaled.

I also wish to thank the Humanities Center of Wayne State University for research support, and the faculty and administration of Wayne State University for supporting the early stages of this project through a Distinguished Faculty Fellowship. And special thanks go to the gifted students in my Images of the Past course, some of whom, including Phil Wagner, will be carrying this work forward. Thanks also to Photofest for providing digital images for reproduction.

Finally, I wish to thank Tova Shaban for her inner fire and outer beauty, and my two sons, Brian and Alex, for their sparkling creativity. I strive, in my own way, to keep up.

INTRODUCTION

As soon as it is formed, the skin of History peels off as film.

André Bazin

The history film has played an exceptionally powerful role in shaping our culture's understanding of the past, an influence that derives not simply from the cinema's unequaled ability to re-create the past in a sensual, mimetic form, but also from its striking tendency to arouse critical and popular controversy that resonates throughout the public sphere. American films centered on the past have often met with a dramatic public response; they typically are both celebrated for their verisimilitude and decried for their departures from accepted historical facts. Historical films have served as vehicles of artistic ambition and as catalysts of public debate from the very beginnings of the art form, as D. W. Griffith's *The Birth of a Nation* (1915) famously illustrates, a tendency that continues into the present day with films such as *JFK* (1991) and *Schindler's List* (1993).

Although much of the public debate concerning history and film has centered on questions of a given film's fidelity to the historical record and its potential to mislead, the historical film has also been recognized for its ability to establish an emotional connection to the past, a connection that can awaken a powerful sense of national belonging or a probing sense of national self-scrutiny. Roland Barthes has said that when watching certain widescreen films, he felt as if he were standing on "the balcony of History," a statement that captures the impressive power of historical films to represent the past from what seems like an ideal vantage point.[1] As a form of narrative interpretation that brings to spectacular life the sweeping themes of the historical past, the Hollywood historical film has played a decisive role in articulating an image of America that informs, or in some cases challenges, our sense of national self-identity, an image of nation that is then projected to the world.

In this book, I examine the characteristics of the American historical film as a specific genre, one that emerged in the earliest days of American filmmaking with Griffith, and that has continued into the present with works by filmmakers such as Oliver Stone, Steven Spielberg, and Clint Eastwood. Like many genres, the historical film has developed several different variants, branching off into distinct subtypes such as the war film, the epic, the biographical film, the topical film, and evolving new, contemporary forms such as the metahistorical film. Although the metahistorical film, which is perhaps best exemplified in the United States by Stone's *JFK*, has emerged only recently, the epic, the war film, and the biographical film emerged more or less at the same time during the silent film period. Although these types of film evolved along distinct paths, what roots them in the larger category of the historical film is their basis in the documentable past, and their shared project of making the world of the past knowable and visible: underpinning the specialized discourses of the epic and the war film, for example, are certain shared conventions of historical representation that serve as rules of engagement for bringing history to the screen.

The historical film has been characterized by Natalie Zemon Davis in a way that provides a useful starting point. She writes that the genre is composed of dramatic feature films in which the primary plot is based on actual historical events, or in which an imagined plot unfolds in such a way that actual historical events are central and intrinsic to the story.[2] This broad, plot-based characterization of the genre captures the specific and unique character of the historical film, which depends for its meaning and significance on an order of events – the historical event – that exists outside the imaginative world of the film itself. However, this definition doesn't take into account the wide variations in the genre, such as films that employ actual historical figures alongside fictional characters, as in *Glory* (1989) and *Braveheart* (1995), or that mix fictional occurrences and actual historical events, such as *Saving Private Ryan* (1999) and *Spartacus* (1960), nor does it take into account the way historical films reshape the past in order to express contemporary concerns, a characteristic that defines much of the critical debate around a film such as *Schindler's List*. Nevertheless, Zemon Davis's description of the historical film serves as a useful, initial demarcation, which is one of the first requirements in specifying a genre. Although I will review and refine this definition during the course of this book, for reasons of pedagogical clarity I feel the succinct characterization provided by Zemon Davis is an effective place to begin.

Within this broad framework, there is a fair amount of variation in the codes and discursive frameworks that govern the way films work to create a historical world. Although several recent books have addressed the ways history is represented in Hollywood films, there has been relatively little written on the historical film as a genre, and the studies that have appeared have had limited value as a guide to the genre's specific characteristics. One exception is Robert Rosenstone's *History on Film/ Film on History*, a work that offers a theoretically informed account of the discursive characteristics of the genre. Rosenstone provides an important perspective on the value of close, sustained analysis of individual works, writing that

> the best of historical films . . . can intersect with, comment upon, and add something to the larger discourse of history out of which they grow and to which they speak . . . By studying what the best historical filmmakers have done, we can come to know better the rules of engagement of the dramatic feature film with the traces of the past.[3]

He also takes much of the existing critical work on historical films to task, pointing out that most studies have been written by historians, rather than from a film studies perspective, and deal principally with a given film's adherence to or deviation from the historical record rather than attempting to come to grips with the way films are structured to create new forms of historical meaning.[4] *Hollywood and History*, in contrast, provides close analyses of some of the most complex and powerful historical films created in Hollywood, and considers the American historical film in all its variants.

The great majority of American films that take the past as their subject can be classified into one of five variant groups: the war film, the biographical film, the epic, the metahistorical film, and the topical film. Together, these five subtypes form a constellation of popular, mainstream films distinguished by their focus on the historical past. I argue that these subtypes, taken as a whole, give us a working model of how history is represented in the American cinema. These different types of film share a common core feature: they are centered on documentable historical events, directly referring to historical occurrences through their main plotlines. Unlike the costume drama or the romance set in the past, history provides the referential content of the historical film. The events of the past constitute the mainspring of the historical film, rather than the past simply serving as a scenic backdrop or a nostalgic setting. By setting these types of films into a theoretical taxonomy, we can begin to see how the past is represented in contemporary culture, and how the style, architecture, social structure, political conflicts and, most importantly, the significant occurrences of the past have been rethought and dramatized in a contemporary idiom.

Both those who love and admire historical films, who appreciate the powerful emotional and perceptual awakening about the past that they produce, as well as those who maintain deep skepticism about the value of popular entertainment as a medium of serious historical reflection, will find reasons to question and challenge the categories I have set out. Many readers will consider my organizing categories to be too few, and will readily find examples of films that engage with the past but that do not fit comfortably into the groups listed above. Other readers may dispute my overall conception in its entirety, and will argue that the historical film does not constitute a genre in the common sense of the word, that the category "historical film" is too nebulous a designation, and that these films do not have the defining stylistic features or the characteristic thematic preoccupations that stamp individual genres. Still other readers may argue that at least three of the subcategories I list above are distinct genres in their own right, and that it serves no critical purpose to propose a new way of approaching these three – the epic, the war film, and the biopic – when they are already perfectly well understood as independent genre forms, and not as subtypes of something larger. These challenges, and others I can imagine, carry considerable weight, and not least because they are direct and commonsensical. To create a taxonomy such as I propose is a little like subjecting films to Hogwarts' sorting hat: sometimes the designation seems odd, and the film seems to resist.

All of these challenges offer valid points for argument and discussion, and are questions that I have asked myself throughout the writing of this book. In the paragraphs below, I provide a summary of my own critical responses to these questions as a way of describing the book, the principal arguments behind it, and the goals that I hope it serves. I foreground three questions as a way of setting out the conceptual foundation for this book. First, the purpose of constructing a taxonomy, and the justification for the categories I employ; second, the issue of whether the historical film constitutes a genre in any meaningful way; and third, whether films should be considered a significant form of historical representation in the first place.

First, the issue of taxonomy. Perhaps the most straightforward argument for a theoretical taxonomy of the historical film is that it provides a critically useful way of approaching the many types of films that have taken the past as their subject. History emerged as a major focus of interest in the American cinema within the first decade of its existence, and with the release of D. W. Griffith's *The Birth of a Nation* in 1915, it became one of the most popular as well as the most controversial forms of cinematic expression. The history of American cinema is replete with serious works of historical imagination, dramatic works that have often opened new windows on the past and have reawakened interest in forgotten figures and particular historical events. Dramatic historical films convey the events of the past in a variety of ways, however, with cinematic style, narrative design, and mode of address defined by specific codes of expression depending on the focus and approach of the film. It is the specific codes that govern how the past is represented in different types of film that I hope to clarify and illustrate through close textual analysis of particular works.

The contemporary period represents one of the most intensive periods of historical film production, and a quick survey of well-regarded and popular works of the contemporary period confirms the validity of the categories that I set out in this book. Many of the most critically acclaimed works of the last fifteen years can be readily identified with one or another of the five categories I propose. For example, the war film is represented by vivid and powerful works such as *Saving Private Ryan* (1995), *Black Hawk Down* (2002), and *Letters from Iwo Jima* (2006). *Nixon* (1995), *Schindler's List* (1993), *The Aviator* (2005), and *Capote* (2005) correspond to the subgenre of the biographical film. *Gladiator* (2000), *Troy* (2004), and *Kingdom of Heaven* (2005) belong to the epic mode. *United 93* (2006), *World Trade Center* (2006), and *Titanic* (1997) can be seen as examples of the topical film. And films such as *JFK* (1990), *Courage Under Fire* (1996), *The New World* (2005), and *Flags of our Fathers* (2006) can be characterized as metahistorical films. These works, as diverse as they are, share a set of common features: they are all either dramatic feature films whose main plotline is based on actual historical events, or they present an imaginary plot that unfolds in such a way that actual historical events are central and intrinsic to the story. Moreover, all of the films listed above convey a strong sense of historical thinking. In keeping with Rosenstone's useful criterion of evaluation, the films listed above attempt to come to grips with the past, making use of the available scholarship and setting out a cinematic interpretation of history that concerns issues that still trouble us in the present.

The second question that has helped to shape my thinking is whether the historical film can be considered a genre in any useful sense, and what good purpose is served by considering the epic, the war film, and the biographical film – forms that are already well established as genres in their own right – as part of something larger. Many critics would limit Hollywood genres to the types of films produced within the classic Hollywood studio system. Others, however, use the term more fluidly, understanding genre as a broadly identifying category, and this is how this book is conceived. Nevertheless, in any serious consideration of individual films, the question of genre is constantly at issue. Particular films are inevitably polysemic, and avail themselves of a range of pre-existing discourses and stylistic borrowings. Poaching, repurposing, and the creation of hybrid forms are the rule of genre, rather than the exception. As Mikhail Bakhtin pointed out with regard to the novel, the dialogical nature of the text, the interweaving of voices, is almost unlimited, a point that has been advanced in film studies by Robert Stam, among others. Even in this context, however, the historical film is a notoriously broad and encompassing category that frequently crosses boundaries. Within the individual films I consider there are frequent contaminations and mixtures of what are usually regarded as fundamentally distinct discourses: for example, the mixture of documentary and constructed sequences of shots in *JFK*, or the combination of heroic biography and the story of the Holocaust in *Schindler's List*.

Nevertheless, genre theory has made great advances in designating and clarifying the characteristics of particular families of films. Some of the most interesting early work in film theory concerned genre, including that of the Russian Formalist Piotrovski on comedy and the later work of Béla Balázs. Recently, Rick Altman has set forth a comprehensive theory of film genre that builds on his earlier, influential work. Altman points out that approaches to film genre have focused on one of two different paradigms for classifying films: they either emphasize the syntax, the narrative and formal patterning of a particular group of works, or they categorize works according to their semantic meanings, the more general traits, settings, and characteristics of the film. To this opposition, he has now added the pragmatic consideration of genre – how texts are mobilized to mean different things for different audiences.[5] Altman's work on the syntactic/semantic/pragmatic interrelationships of genre forms is complex and nuanced, and I do not have space to explicate it here. However, this model has helped me think through the issues involved in historical representation in film.

As elastic as the concept of genre is, the syntactic understanding of genre would seem to be stretched beyond recognition if we were to look for common structural, narrative, or formal characteristics among films as diverse as *JFK, Saving Private Ryan, Schindler's List,* and *United 93* – all films that I treat in detail in the chapters that follow. What Altman calls the genre's "fundamental syntax . . . the relationships linking the lexical elements" – the syntactic approach – can be understood as the narrative patterning of a particular genre, the combinations that structure the unfolding of the narrative.[6] Interesting and useful work has been done on the syntax of particular genres, including the war film and the biographical film. For the purposes of designating a genre affiliation, the syntactic approach, applied in isolation from other considerations, would find that the war film and the biographical film are clearly separate forms, with specific narrative combinations and plot sequences. Moreover, a distinct syntax marks each of the different types of film that I propose to group under the heading of the historical. At the syntactic level, the epic and the war film, the biographical film, and the topical film are distinct. To try to cobble them together in one category would be to construct a chimera, an impossible beast.

The alternative approach to defining genre is the semantic approach, which stresses, in Altman's words, the "common traits, attitudes, characters . . . the building blocks of the genre."[7] The semantic approach is broad and inclusive, emphasizing atmosphere, stock characters, and setting, unlike the syntactical which is exclusive, and works on only a small corpus of films. The semantic approach emphasizes the "narrative world" constructed by the genre, the relation of sign to world, rather than the unfolding of narrative combinations. And here, we can find a point of connection among the films I treat in this study, for they are all films that are centered on reenacting the past.

What brings these different orders of representation – the epic, the war film, the biographical film, and the topical film – into the same discursive framework is the concept of reenactment, the act of imaginative re-creation that allows the spectator to imagine they are "witnessing again" the events of the past. The principle of reenactment constitutes the semantic register of the genre. The historical film conveys its messages about the world by reenacting the past, and it is the idea of reenactment that provides its semantic ground.

In reenacting the past, the Hollywood historical film employs a variety of techniques to produce a heightened sense of fidelity and verisimilitude, creating a powerfully immersive experience for the spectator. Many of the characteristic features of the historical film directly function to reinforce the experiential core of the genre, its impression of "witnessing again." Roland Barthes is eloquent on this point. In his short essay, "On Cinemascope," he describes the "stretched-out frontality" of the widescreen image as

> the ideal space of the great dramaturgies . . . Imagine yourself in front of *Battleship Potemkin*, no longer stationed at the end of a telescope but supported by the same air, the same stone, the same crowd: this ideal Potemkin, where you could finally join hands with the insurgents, share the same light, and experience the tragic Odessa Steps in their fullest force, this is what is now possible; the balcony of History is ready. What remains to be seen is what we'll be shown there.[8]

His description of the plenary amplitude, the somatic intensity of the cinematic experience, especially the sense of rewitnessing the historical past, is a vivid reminder of the primacy of reenactment in the historical film.

In addition to creating a powerful impression of "witnessing again," the reenactment involves a form of double consciousness, a rethinking of the past. Reenacting the past necessarily calls forth the historical imagination on the part of the filmmaker and the film spectator. As Paul Ricoeur writes, "re-enacting does not consist in re-living but in rethinking, and rethinking already contains the critical moment that forces us to take the detour by way of the historical imagination."[9] Rather than a simple re-experiencing, as if there were no gap between the actual event and its re-presentation, the filmmaker and the spectator alike project themselves into a past world in order to reimagine it, to perform it, and to rethink it. The role of the historical imagination in historical reenactment justifies, and perhaps even requires the use of diverse materials and different orders of discourse.

The reimagining of the past takes shape through particular stylistic and narrative devices in film, generating a range of historical styles, from the realism of Roberto Rossellini to the cinematic *écriture* of Sergei Eisenstein. The array of styles, subjects, and approaches in the Hollywood historical film can be understood as the syntactic register of the historical film, a syntax that is expressed in the form of the war film, the epic, or the biographical film. By analyzing the particular syntax employed by the war film, for example, the structural and formal elements of this particular type of film are set in relief. The specific textual unfolding of *Saving Private Ryan*, for example, comes from an established lexicon of narrative moves, and from the variations and new combinations it creates. The underlying premise of the film, however, what might be called the point of the film, is the concept of reenactment, the impression it creates of "witnessing again."

The historical film takes shape through the interplay of these two registers, the syntactic and the semantic. In this book I move between these two emphases, the syntactic and the semantic, understanding their complementary and interactive character, taking advantage of the strengths of each type of approach, and showing, where possible, how they interrelate. I also explore the way particular audiences have appropriated specific films to produce their own reading communities, a point that is particularly evident in the audience responses to *Schindler's List*, *Saving Private Ryan*, and *Gladiator*.

The third question I have asked myself is in some ways the most fundamental one: Why should dramatic fiction films be considered a medium of historical reflection in the first place? What is gained by analyzing films such as *Spartacus* or *Schindler's List* as examples of "historical thinking"? Several historians, including Rosenstone, Zemon Davis, Hayden White, and Robert Toplin, have addressed this issue, and found much to recommend the cinema as a medium of historical interpretation. Rosenstone is certainly the most sanguine about dramatic fiction film as a form of history. He writes that "film is not history in our traditional sense, but it is a kind of history nonetheless . . . films give us tools to see reality in a new way – including the realities of a past which has long since vanished from our sight."[10] Arguing that certain filmmakers should be considered historians, he suggests that film might be understood as a "new form of historical thinking," that film "gives us a new form of history, what we might call history as vision."[11]

Even Rosenstone, however, seems uneasy about the fictional aspect of historical films, the fact that they are not "always built on blocks of verifiable data" as properly historical narrative requires, the fact that invention plays such a major role in the film's construction of the past. The use of invention may require that the word "history" be removed from the dramatic fiction film, he writes, but not the notions of "historical thinking" and "historical understanding," particularly if the film is engaged with historical issues, contests existing interpretations, or uncovers stories or chapters from the past that have been suppressed in the dominant accounts.

It is this uneasiness with the fictional aspect of dramatic historical films that has led many theorists and historians to argue from a "presentist" position. For these writers, including the influential historian Pierre Sorlin, historical films can provide historical knowledge only about the period in which they were made. The past in historical films becomes an allegory of the present; the milieu in which the film was produced stamps every frame.[12] An example is the thorough and careful study of the various film versions of *Spartacus* set forth by Maria Wyke. The several films of the story of Spartacus, first distributed in the United States in 1914, display markedly different visions of the main character. Wyke demonstrates the shaping influence of the present on the images of the past in a close study of three films made in different periods and different national settings. In her treatment, Spartacus is shown to be a chameleon-like historical figure, a quality that is facilitated by the paucity of ancient documents relating to him and the slave rebellion he led. In the culminating 1960 version by Stanley Kubrick, she locates the decisive role that the context of 1950s America played in molding the vision of the film. Spartacus started out in Howard Fast's and Dalton Trumbo's written versions as a leftist revolutionary, and wound up as a "Cold War warrior" battling for Christian freedom against pagan Rome, which served as a stand-in for the Soviet Union. Here, the Red Scare, the Black List, the Cold War, and even the potential for a more liberal worldview were all manifestly present in the portrayal of the past the film presents.[13]

Others insist that the historical film is of greatest value when it "lets the past be the past," and that the foreignness and "otherness" of the past must be respected.[14] Zemon Davis's reading of Kubrick's *Spartacus* discloses a film that is thoroughly imbued with the values, perspectives, and familial codes of the ancient past. Reading the extensive correspondence between screenwriter Trumbo and Kubrick, she discerns a deep engagement with the issues that concern historians, and a full consideration of the risks involved in modernizing the story. Although the filmmakers fall short of a genuinely historical portrayal, the film shows the potential for films to bring to life an ancient, quite alien world.[15] The value of the historical film for Zemon Davis resides in its ability to serve as a kind of "thought experiment" about the past, an imaginative activity that allows us to leave the present behind, to project ourselves into a world that is not stamped by our habitual social understandings and our programmed sense of sexuality, family, religion, and interpersonal relations. Film, better than any other medium, can provide a vivid experience and a powerful emotional relationship with a world that is wholly unfamiliar. To employ another vocabulary, historical film can defamiliarize our image of the past.

The historical film, like the mythic figure of Janus, looks both to the past and the present. On the one hand, Hollywood historical films carefully and insistently cultivate a sense that they faithfully represent the past, in some cases by using documentary images of the actual occurrences and figures, as in *JFK*, or by creating extremely realistic and authentic reconstructions of battles, as in *Saving Private Ryan*, or simply, as Martin Scorsese says of *Gangs of New York*, by creating an "impression of a world."[16] On the other hand, every historical film constructs the past in a way that is shaped and informed by its own context, its own way of imagining the past.

The historical film can be distinguished by this dual focus. By reenacting the past in the present, the historical film brings the past into dialogue with the present. The critical interest of this genre of films lies precisely in the juxtaposition of old and new, the powerful sense that what is being rendered on-screen is not an imaginary world, but a once-existing world that is being reinscribed in an original way. Vigorous discussions concerning authenticity, historical truth, and artistic interpretation are provoked by this dual orientation, which provides the genre with one of its richest sources of critical discourse. In my view, it is the dialogue between these two sets of perspectives that defines the historical film. Like a hologram, it appears to contain two perspectives, two vantage points on the past in a single form. The dual perspectives of the historical film allow for openness in the definition of the genre. At the same time, this dual focus suggests certain limits as well. The principle of reenactment implies that the event being revisited actually did occur, but it also implies that this event still has meaning for us in the present.

Recent debates about whether the telling of the past on screen counts as "historical thinking" provide a standard and a provisional set of criteria for determining the films to be discussed and the analytic approach that I employ. Although many films set in the past can be considered historical in some aspect or another, the taxonomy I propose is limited to films that foreground historical events in a recognizable way. Although costume dramas and romances set in the past, as exemplified by films like *Dangerous Liaisons* (1988) and *Age of Innocence* (1993), are aesthetically intriguing works, and critical analysis of these films would undoubtedly reveal much that is deeply historical in terms of setting, costume, and class behavior, the criteria that to me seem most relevant in specifying the genre of historical films are largely absent from these films: the sense of "historical thinking" that the works communicate, and the degree to which actual historical events have an impact on the plot.

In this book, I explore the way the way historical films shape our concept of the past through the specific languages and codes of the cinema, using close textual analysis to disclose the way images and sounds create a particular form of historical thinking. Although the historical film emerged in the first decades of the cinema, the specific characteristics of form and structure have scarcely been considered. The messages we take from these films, which are certainly among the most important cultural artifacts of the past century, are communicated by the editing, cinematography, lighting, sound, and narrative design of these works, elements that convey an interpretation of the past that is nuanced and complex.

I begin by surveying the genre of the American historical film from its beginnings, which can be traced to the first decade of film production in the United States, to the present day. Several works by Edison and Porter that feature depictions of what was at the time the recent past point to a powerful early interest in the representation of historical events on film. In addition, I discuss the prehistory of the genre, represented by numerous forms of popular entertainment and instruction such as historical tableaus, dioramas, and panoramas that can be seen as direct antecedents of the historical film. In the half-century preceding the invention of the cinema, for example, large-scale paintings of historical events in the form of panoramas, sometimes staged in a 360-degree format, and sometimes with the added cinematic effect of movement, were especially popular. Several of the 360-degree panoramas featured changing canvas panels that allowed reenactments of historical events to unfold over a period of hours, foreshadowing the epic style of presentation of many historical films.

The overview will extend from the prehistory of the genre, through the silent period and the classic studio years, to the resurgence of the genre in the Hollywood cinema emblematically represented by the work of Oliver Stone, Steven Spielberg, and Clint Eastwood. In this chapter, I will delineate the five main subtypes of the historical film and discuss their development.

Although the historical feature film dates from D. W. Griffith's *The Birth of a Nation* in 1915, and numerous one- and two-reel short films dedicated to historical subjects appeared before that, the exceptional number of serious historical films that have been produced in the contemporary period suggests that the genre is now entering a defining and exemplary era. The films that I have selected for chapter-length analyses, therefore, are recent films that illuminate the genre, and the history of the genre, by reworking and revising motifs and themes that have been employed in historical filmmaking from the earliest periods of film. The five individual chapters that form the core of the book will center on contemporary examples of the five main types of historical film. Although I will focus, with two exceptions, on only one film in each chapter, I will use the film under discussion as a springboard to consider a range of other films of the same type from earlier and from the contemporary periods.

I begin by analyzing the role of the war film, exemplified by *Saving Private Ryan*, as a major vehicle of national self-definition and as an important catalyst for technological innovation in film. *Saving Private Ryan* illustrates the distinctive connection between the historical film and other activities of organized remembering. Drawing on and encapsulating a widespread cultural fervor of remembrance for what has been called the "greatest generation," the film dramatizes in an exceptionally powerful way the events that stand out in American popular consciousness – the D-day landings – as emblematic of the American war effort. The film's unique contribution to the culture of commemoration that has developed around the veterans of World War II is in its amplified appeal to empathy and emotion, an amplification that, I argue, is fostered by its cinematography and special effects.

Celebrated for the authenticity of its battlefield sequences as well as for its powerful evocation of nostalgia for the certainties of the "last good war," the film resurrected the traditional war film, which had fallen into disrepute in the post-Vietnam period, and reestablished it as a dominant form in American cinema. Following on the success of *Saving Private Ryan*, several traditional war films have been released to marked box-office and some critical success, films such as *Black Hawk Down* and *Letters from Iwo Jima* (2006). In rehearsing and reinvigorating the genre motifs and conventions of the war films of the past, however, *Saving Private Ryan* also broke new ground in its technological innovations. Much of its success was based on its special effects, most evident in the Omaha Beach landing sequence, in which the film blends computer-generated imagery, live action photography, reenactments of documentary photographs and sequences, accelerated editing, slow-motion cinematography, and electronically enhanced sound design – in other words, its use of postmodern strategies of pastiche and fragmentary narration. Through the use of open-ended and destabilizing visual techniques, the film establishes a powerful claim to battlefield authenticity and realism, a claim that has been buttressed by the supporting testimony of D-day veterans concerning the accuracy of the film's depiction of combat. *Saving Private Ryan* thus combines a traditional, veridical interpretation of the past – an interpretation that stresses the importance of the individual soldier and the success of the collective endeavor mounted on his behalf – with advanced visual and acoustic techniques that are usually considered postmodern.

The film's innovative use of technology places it in a long tradition of war films that have broken new ground in terms of special effects, creative camerawork, and mass choreography in the service of realism and emotional power. *The Longest Day* (1962), *All Quiet on the Western Front* (1930), and *The Birth of a Nation* (1915), for example, all established new camera and optical techniques, and set new standards for realism in film. The striking combination of emotionally charged subject matter and innovative cinematic technique gives the war film a potent role in forging a sense of national identity and national cohesion.

In the following chapter, I analyze the rewriting of genre codes in *Spartacus* and *Gladiator*, both of which were considered radical departures, at the time of their release, from the epic mode. Both films exemplify the role of "genre memory," a concept set forth by Mikhail Bakhtin, in shaping the way the past is reenacted, illustrating the way genre forms recall past usages while making their resources available for the present.[17] Although the epic film is notably more inventive in its interpretation of historical events than other forms of historical film, the epic embodies, in the view of Gilles Deleuze, a strikingly coherent historical approach, one that he likens to classic nineteenth-century German historiography. In this tradition, the historical world is rendered through the orchestration of three critical modes – the monumental; the antiquarian; and the critical-ethical, a style of rendering the past embodied in contemporary life by the Hollywood historical epic. In employing these three perspectives, the epic film creates a striking expression of what Deleuze calls "universal history"; here, each major historical epoch displays similar characteristics, visible in certain traits, architectural motifs, and the pattern of their historical ascent and decline. Each displays the taint of decadence as well as the ferment of new life. The American epic film replays this universal story, finding in every epic story a pattern of decadence, decline, and the germs of new life, a story that is completed in the quintessential American story of the "birth of a nation." In the epic film, Hollywood communicates "via the peaks" with the great civilizations of the past, a theme that is nicely illustrated in the closing shots of *The Ten Commandments*, as Moses stands on a mountain ledge with his hand raised in farewell, holding a sacred scroll in his other hand, a pose that directly recalls the Statue of Liberty.

In many ways, *Spartacus* and *Gladiator* both rehearse the historiographic approach outlined by Deleuze, but in other ways, they depart from convention to seize on contemporary cultural perspectives, expressing Cold War political concerns, in the case of *Spartacus*, or conveying the dualistic nature of imperialism in *Gladiator*, a form of imperial domination one critic has called "soft hegemony." The epic draws from the genre memory of the past while at the same time expressing new possibilities of cultural identification and belonging. Epic films express not only "what did occur," but also what "might have occurred," and thus present a particularly striking example of the influence of the contemporary context on forms of historical representation.

Although the epic had been in decline for several decades – a period described by one critic as the time of "the incredibly shrinking epic" – it has reasserted itself strongly with films such as *Gladiator, Kingdom of Heaven* (2005), *Braveheart* (1995), and *Troy* (2004). One writer has said that "true film epics can only be made at a time when a country's national myths are still believed – or, at best, when a nation feels itself slipping into decline, which produces a spate of nostalgic evocations of those myths."[18] Reading *Spartacus* and *Gladiator* in relation to one another provides an opportunity to consider the relation between the reemergence of the epic form and the cultural, social, and political context of the present period, and to reflect on the relations of present-day Hollywood and earlier periods in American filmmaking when the epic genre prevailed as a strong form.

Another issue I consider in this chapter is the way films set in ancient Rome have become part of the historical capital of twentieth-century US culture. Hollywood's Roman history films are in many ways an extension of a long tradition of borrowing from the Roman past in order to crystallize and critique aspects of American national identity. From the founding years of the nation-state, the imagery of ancient Rome was deployed to link the civic ideals of the fledgling nation to the classical past with its ready-made connotations of democracy, liberty, a nd nobility. George Washington, for example, was frequently pictured in Roman garb, and the architecture of Washington, DC is modeled on the Roman forum.[19] However, Rome was also identified with decadence and opulence, and many early commentators at various points compared the likely fate of the United States to the ultimate fate of the Roman Empire. Hollywood films set in Rome, such as *Ben Hur*,

Quo Vadis (1951), and *The Robe* (1953) often exploited the ambiguities and contradictions associated with ancient Rome as a site of both ideal civic virtue as well as decadent excess to express the social iniquities within the United States itself.

Schindler's List is a powerful exemplar of the continuing importance of the biographical film. In this chapter, I also briefly consider *Citizen Kane* (1941), *Nixon* (1995), and the biographical films produced by David O. Selznick in the 1930s. The biographical film, or biopic, is perhaps the most familiar form of cinematic historiography: it is by far the largest subgenre of historical filmmaking. For the most part, however, the biographical film has been seen as a conservative, mainstream form, an aesthetic embarrassment; as Barthes says about biography in general, it is "the fiction that dare not speak its name."[20] Nevertheless, pathfinding films such as *Malcolm X* (1992), *Nixon*, *The Aviator* (2005) and, by some accounts, *Citizen Kane* render the lives of their characters in a modernist, cubist style, emphasizing the ambiguity, the complexity, and the multiple dimensions of an individual life. In this chapter, I approach *Schindler's List* as a an example of a modernist biographical film, a work that reaches back to what Miriam Hansen calls "vernacular modernism" to express, in a popular idiom, a thematically complex work rendered in an advanced visual and acoustic style.

In *Schindler's List*, the codes and conventions familiar from the biographical film tradition are transformed. Rather than being defined in a typical way as an exemplary figure of his age, or alternatively, as an original man of genius, Schindler is a figure whose vices and weaknesses are the most pronounced aspects of the character we view. A con man and serial seducer, Schindler uses his Nazi Party connections to create a successful business, with free labor supplied by the Jewish workers. But in the vastly more criminal world of Nazi Poland, Schindler's flaws become his strengths. As one critic says, he is a true Brechtian character; his faults become his strengths, transformed by the context into positive virtues. Here, character is determined by the social milieu.

Schindler's List brings into relief many of the most pointed and difficult questions concerning the Hollywood historical film. It purports to represent an event that for many historians and scholars is considered unrepresentable; it tells the story of the Holocaust from the perspective of a German businessman, a member of the Nazi Party, and it narrates this event in a cinematic idiom in which a story of mass extinction is dramatized through the actions of a charismatic individual. In this chapter, I analyze *Schindler's List* as a film that illustrates both the strengths and limitations of narrating history by following the trajectory of an individual life. One of the questions I pursue is whether the biographical historical film can reveal the complexities of history, or whether its focus on the individual agent as the crystallized expression of historical forces compromises its power of historical explanation. Does the story of an individual character dedicated to a life of fashion and pleasure, who gradually becomes an authentic moral agent leading a heroic rescue, falsify and distort the historical past? Or does *Schindler's List* rather illustrate the value of mainstream film as a vehicle of public memory, a form of mass-mediated memory that is genuinely public and collective? As Miriam Hansen writes, "We need to understand the place of Schindler's List in the contemporary culture of memory and memorializing; and the film in turn may help us understand that culture."[21]

In Chapter 5 I analyze the film *JFK* as a highly charged example of the metahistorical film, a type of film that interrogates the way history is traditionally represented. *JFK* performs a powerful critique of the "consensual reality" produced in American culture by the media, taking the media's own images and defamiliarizing them by placing them in new contexts. The film presents a provocative interpretation of the assassination of John F. Kennedy in a highly charged, polemical style that mixes idioms, splices together documentary and fictional footage, and uses montage editing to disorient and "agitate" the viewer in a manner that calls into question accepted interpretations of the past. *JFK* is an emblematic example a style of filmmaking that takes a postmodern approach to the representation of the past, one that falls into the film category that Rosenstone calls "revisioning" history.

Rosenstone divides historical films into three general categories: those that "vision" history – films that present a traditional, experiential representation of the past in a more or less realist framework; those that "contest" history and that challenge the metanarratives that structure historical knowledge; and those that "revision" history, films that reject the realism that purports to show the world "as it is" in favor of "expressive modes of representation that expand the vocabulary of the historian," such as those in *JFK*.[22] An accomplished and controversial work, *JFK* contests not only the official accounts of Kennedy's assassination, aided and supported by the media, which became a pervasive influence following Kennedy's assassination, but also the traditional realism of the historical film, placing pressure on the codes and conventions by which history is represented in the cinema. Although there are strong traditions of radically innovative approaches to historical filmmaking in other national cinemas – one thinks immediately of the Soviet cinema, the New Latin American cinema, and various European cinemas – there are few examples of stylistically innovative historical films to date in the United States. Works such as *Nixon, Courage Under Fire* (1996), *Three Kings* (1999), *The New World* (2005), and *Flags of Our Fathers* (2006) are a few of the other works that correspond to this category. I discuss the postmodern historical film not as an established subgenre, but rather as a form, whose prototype is *JFK*, that may point the way for future developments in the genre.

Finally, in Chapter 6 I discuss two major dramatic films about 9/11, *United 93* (2006) and *World Trade Center*, as examples of the topical film. Many historical films depict a single event as a way of illuminating the larger currents of history, or dramatize an episode in the past that that sheds particular light on a specific period. Films such as *Titanic, Rosewood, The Mission, Eight Men Out*, and *The Long Walk Home* can be considered topical works, films that crystallize historical issues and conflicts through the lens of a particular event. In *United 93* and *World Trade Center*, the transformative event of 9/11 is considered in a rigorously minimalist way; both films maintain a focus that zeroes in on specific, individual experiences, foregoing the wider contextual analyses of films such as *JFK*. These self-imposed limitations, the refusal to set the event within a larger interpretive context, can be read in two ways. On the one hand, each work holds rigorously to a narrative arc that emphasizes human agency and collective heroic action in the face of overwhelming catastrophe. Sensitive to the demand that representations of 9/11 have a special connection to "discourses of responsibility," the films rehearse a pattern that has emerged as a culturally dominant formula, underscoring the theme of heroism in a much larger landscape of loss, ruin, and victimization. Each film reenacts the event as closely as possible, "re-witnessing" the tragedy by framing it as a narrative of heroic agency. On the other hand, the close, almost obsessive rehearsal of individual experiences in these works can be seen as a form of traumatic response, an obsessive revisiting of the scene of the injury, an inability to narrate and interpret the event in an ongoing narrative of cultural significance. Nowhere in *United 93* or *World Trade Center* are the compound contexts, the traumatic cultural and social effects, the devastating losses, or the profound alterations of national life that characterize 9/11 registered. Instead, linear narrative patterning and classical limitations of character, place, and temporality impose a rigorous and singular structure. The dramatic organization of both works suggests a kind of fixation or obsession, a determined refusal to acknowledge the radical alteration of national life wrought by 9/11.

The two films emblematically express a fragmentary, atomized sense of information coming partially and too late, the loss of an overarching, transcendent vision, the collapse of seemingly reliable systems for managing and comprehending events. At the same time, they powerfully evoke the sustaining value of narratives of heroism, offering a narrative framework to render events that cannot yet be assimilated in the wider culture. They offer a glimpse of "how traumatic traces of history seep or break through the triumphant, heroic narrative."[23] These two works provide an opportunity to discuss an emerging critical discourse drawn from trauma studies. Here, I offer a reading of these films as poised between two moments of traumatic response, between the obsessive repetition of the event, "acting out," and the therapeutic process of "working through." I also consider the films in the light of Japanese cinematic and artistic responses to Hiroshima, a mode of representation that may provide certain insights into emerging forms of 9/11 imaging.

Throughout the book, certain ideas about the historical film appear frequently enough to form a set of motifs or common themes. These ideas, some of which I summarize below, link all of the films I discuss, and offer, I think, a sense of the significance of the genre for the larger culture. Beyond the artistic and historiographic accomplishments of particular films, the major issues of history, memory, representation, and cultural identity resonate throughout the genre. In every decade, certain films seem to challenge the culture's wider understanding of itself, and in every decade, the importance of historical cinema makes itself felt in terms of controversy, passionate enthusiasm, and broad public debate. And the afterlife of historical filmmaking is exceptionally long. The cultural significance of films like *The Birth of a Nation*, *All Quiet on the Western Front*, *Spartacus*, *Glory*, and *Schindler's List* is renewed with each decade. Certain historical films link past and present in a way that allows a national dialogue to unfold, one that links different generations of viewers and different periods of critical response, and that ultimately reaches back to the reference period of the film itself. These works become part of the public sphere in ways that only a few artistic artifacts can claim. Among the themes that are woven through this study are the following:

1. *The relationship between historical films and an emerging or changing understanding of national identity.* The most prominent examples of the genre, works such as *The Birth of a Nation*, *All Quiet on the Western Front*, *Spartacus*, *Saving Private Ryan*, *Glory*, and *JFK*, coincide with or in some cases catalyze larger cultural debates about national identity and national belonging. The historical film often brings into

relief the complex cultural and political context of the period in which it is made, a characteristic that is amply demonstrated in the charged and polarized reception given to a film such as *JFK*. Films that set out to dramatize or ask questions about the past frequently arouse intensive debate and discussion about the meaning of nation and history. These debates provide a useful way of considering the films in their cultural context.

2. *The link between historical films and other forms of organized remembering.* One of the distinguishing features of the genre is the intensive commemorative activity that often attends the release of a historical film. *Glory*, for example, elicited a number of genealogical projects and reenactments by black descendants of Civil War soldiers, and spawned a host of related cultural activities such as exhibitions, ballets, and republications dedicated to remembering the contributions of black soldiers during the Civil War. A similar collective project of remembering circulated around *Saving Private Ryan* and the HBO series, *Band of Brothers*. Certain historical films have become focal points for expressions of public memory, for the revitalization of ethnic and racial traditions, and for creative projects in other media. The genre thus intersects with concepts of national and ethnic heritage in ways that lend these films a particular salience as cultural artifacts.

3. *The historical film as a vehicle of artistic ambition and studio prestige.* Many historical films have been heavily promoted as prestigious cultural events. The studio publicity surrounding historical films confers a sense of grandeur on the films that often results in Academy Awards, endorsements by leading cultural and political figures, and occasionally, a backlash in the form of protests and editorial denunciations. As a genre, the historical film has been both valorized for its cultural importance and denigrated for its commercial orientation. These films bring into relief competing ideas about cultural value, prestige, and commercial success that typically surround major historical films.

Notes

1 Roland Barthes, "On CinemaScope," trans. Jonathan Rosenbaum. First published in *Les lettres nouvelles*, February 1954. Accessed at *http://social.chass.ncsu.edu/jouvert/v3i3/barth.htm*. James Morrison comments on Barthes's very short essay in the companion piece, "On Barthes On CinemaScope."

2 Natalie Zemon Davis, *Slaves on Screen: Film and Historical Vision* (Cambridge, MA: Harvard University Press, 2000).

3   Robert Rosenstone, *History on Film/Film on History* (Harlow, England and New York: Pearson Education, 2006): 31.

4   See Trevor McCrisken and Andrew Pepper, *American History and Contemporary Hollywood Film*; Robert Brent Toplin, *Reel History: In Defense of Hollywood*; Susan E. Linville, *History Films, Women, and Freud's Uncanny*; William Guynn, *Writing History in Film*; J. David Slocum, ed., *Hollywood and War: The Film Reader*; and Robert Eberwein, ed., *The War Film*.

5   See Herbert Eagle, *Russian Formalist Film Theory* (Ann Arbor: Slavic Publications, 1982).

6   Rick Altman, *Film/Genre* (London: British Film Institute, 1999): 219–220.

7   Ibid.: 219.

8   Barthes, "On CinemaScope." See also James Morrison's illuminating commentary on this very short essay, "On Barthes On Cinemascope."

9   Paul Ricoeur, *The Reality of the Historical Past* (Milwaukee, WI: Marquette University Press, 1984): 8.

10 Rosenstone, *History on Film*: 158.

11 Ibid.: 163, 160.

12 Pierre Sorlin, *The Film in History: Restaging the Past* (Totowa, NJ: Barnes & Noble, 1980).

13 Maria Wyke, *Projecting the Past: Ancient Rome, Cinema, and History* (London: Routledge, 1997): 34–72.

14 Zemon Davis, *Slaves on Screen*: 136.

15 See Natalie Zemon Davis, "Trumbo and Kubrick Argue History," *Raritan* 22:1 (2002): 173–90, and *Slaves on Screen*: 17–40.

16 Martin Scorsese, "Manhattan Asylum," interview with Ian Christie, *Sight and Sound*, January 2003.

17 For a discussion of the concept of "genre memory," see Gary Saul Morson and Caryl Emerson, *Mikhail Bakhtin: The Creation of a Prosaics* (Stanford, CA: Stanford University Press, 1990). See also Robert Burgoyne, *Film Nation: Hollywood Looks at U.S. History* (Minneapolis: University of Minnesota Press, 1997) for an application of this concept to film.

18 Allan Barra quotes the British critic Paul Coates in "The Incredible Shrinking Epic," *American Film* 14:5 (1989): 40–5.

19 See Wyke, *Projecting the Past*: 1–33.

20 Barthes, quoted in Rosenstone, *History on Film*: 91.

21 Miriam Hansen, "*Schindler's List* Is Not *Shoah*: Second Commandment, Popular Modernism, and Public Memory," in Yosefa Loshitzky, ed., *Spielberg's Holocaust: Critical Perspectives on Schindler's List* (Bloomington: Indiana University Press, 1997): 77–103.

22 Robert Rosenstone, ed., "Introduction," in *Revisioning History: Film and the Construction of a New Past* (Princeton, NJ: Princeton University Press, 1995): 3–13.

23 E. Ann Kaplan and Ban Wang, eds., "Introduction," in *Trauma and Cinema Cross-Cultural Explorations* (Hong Kong: Hong Kong University Press, 2004): 15.

CHAPTER 1

THE CINEMATIC WRITING OF HISTORY: AN OVERVIEW

Beginning with D. W. Griffith's *The Birth of a Nation* in 1915, the historical film has been one of the most celebrated forms of cinematic expression as well as one of the most controversial. As a genre, it has maintained a high degree of cultural prominence over a period of almost a hundred years, and it has established itself as a major form in nearly every nation that produces films. But it has also consistently provoked controversy and widespread public debate about the meaning of the past, about the limits of dramatic interpretation, and about the power of film to influence popular understanding and to promote particular national myths.

The historical film has often served as a vehicle of studio prestige and artistic ambition, and many distinguished directors have made major contributions to the genre. In recent years, directors such as Steven Spielberg, Martin Scorsese, Oliver Stone, Clint Eastwood, John Sayles, Edward Zwick, Bernardo Bertolucci, and Roman Polanski have made important and powerful historical films that have reawakened interest in aspects of the past that were not previously well represented or understood. For many societies, the historical film now serves as the dominant source of popular knowledge about the historical past, a fact that has made some professional historians anxious. Other historians, however, see these films as valuable for the discussions and debate they generate. Films such as *Schindler's List* (1993) and *JFK* (1991), for example, have fostered a widespread and substantial public discussion that has contributed to historical appreciation and understanding.

The Beginnings of the Historical Film

One of the earliest forms of widescreen historical reenactment was the panorama, a spectacular 360-degree circular representation that combined special lighting, sound effects, music, narration, and sometimes movement to produce a full sensory experience, an early form of sensual immersion for the pre-cinematic audience. One of several spectacular forms of mechanical illusionism that emerged in the nineteenth century, the panorama played a special role as a form of historical representation.[1] In a century that seemed to be obsessed with the dream of lifelike visual reproduction, the panorama was a popular form of visual entertainment, rendering battlefield scenes, shipwrecks, and dramatic scenes of historical events such as the burning of the Houses of Parliament or the Coronation of King George IV. As Alison Griffiths writes, "the locations and events painted by panoramists had to resonate as suitable subjects for the epic mode of representation: 'big subjects for big pictures.'"[2] Spectators, sometimes situated on a raised platform in the center of the panorama, received an early experience of an immersive environment in which verisimilitude and authenticity were emphasized. Certain panoramas made such an impression on spectators that they were deemed inappropriate for women and children, with the publicity of the day suggesting that only the most stalwart males would be able to defend themselves against the vertiginous impression of what appeared to be an actual wreck at sea or the experience of explosive carnage on the water. Adding to the "reality effect" of these spectaculars was the added attraction of actual movement: some famous panoramas mounted their painted canvas scenes on enormous rollers, scrolling the painting in front of the viewers to produce movement and a continuously changing vista. The panorama of the journey down the Mississippi River constructed by John Banvard, for example, a special type of river panorama, was advertised as being three miles long.[3] The scale of these works – the panorama of the Battle of Gettysburg, for example, is some 20,000 square feet in size – the use of theatrical lighting and the sensational nature of the scenes they depicted suggest that these works had much in common with the epic scale of historical films.[4]

Theatrical producers copied the effects of the panorama by incorporating moving backgrounds into certain plays. The early stage productions of *Ben-Hur: A Tale of the Christ*, for example, staged the climactic chariot race with real horses pulling as many as seven chariots on stage, creating a spectacular impression of movement and drama. The teams of horses, four to each chariot, ran on individual treadmills situated just beneath the stage. The come-from-behind victory of Ben-Hur was engineered by having his treadmill physically moved from below the stage by a group of men to the lead position. The treadmills of the other chariots, including that of his enemy Messala, were then moved backward. Augmenting the impression of speed was a moving background of the Circus Maximus, an enormous painted scene of Roman spectators in the arena, a background that was whipped across the back of the stage by two enormous rollers at a speed of thirty miles per hour.[5]

Panoramas also served as an early form of newsreel, visualizing recent events of national importance, military victories, naval battles, and the like. People were eager to rewitness the most recent events occurring in faraway places, and panoramas served this role in a period when a breaking news story might take two months to be reported. Major panoramas were painted in as little as one week.

Cinema in the United States received a tremendous boost in popularity with the Spanish-American War in 1898. The public had a keen interest in seeing images of the war, and filmmakers responded by providing facsimiles or reenactments that they passed off as authentic eyewitness accounts. The "newsreel" films of these events, however, were entirely staged, as the difficulty of getting cameramen to the sites of battles and naval engagements made on-the-spot location shooting impossible. Instead, scenes were reenacted for the camera, often in a primitive studio. For example, the sinking of the *Maine*, one of the most well-known and contested events of the war, was represented in a film, *The Battle of Manila Bay*, by J. Stuart Blackton, with scale models set up in a bathtub. Edison and the Biograph Company, unable to get footage of the *Maine*, used earlier footage of the battleships *Massachusetts* and *Iowa* and simply renamed the film *Battleships Maine and Iowa*. And the climactic victory over the Spanish, emblematized in the short film *Raising Old Glory Over Morro Castle*, consisted of a staged action in front of an obviously painted backdrop. Even George Meliès, the master of early special effects, contributed to the emerging war-film genre with an underwater shot of the *Maine* explosion, staged in an aquarium. All of these fabricated works were presented as "eyewitness accounts."[6]

The public responded to these early war films in vast numbers; very short works dealing with the Spanish–American War were often the highlight of vaudeville programs, and were presented with patriotic songs and music. The popularity of the war in general, which was enthusiastically promoted throughout American media culture, gave the public a reason to pay attention to the cinema. The consensus among historians of early cinema is that the Spanish–American War fueled the public's interest in film at a time when the industry was just beginning to establish itself, a time when its future was by no means certain. James Castonguay writes that the film-producing companies of the day were literally transformed into "signifying war machines." Edison, for example, renamed his Projecting Kinetoscope the "Wargraph," and other film companies followed suit with names like the "Warscope." Cinema's role as a medium of historical representation was established with these works; as early as 1898, the war film became a major form of cinematic expression.[7]

Apart from these early war films, other historical subjects also drew the interest of filmmakers. Titles such as *The Execution of Mary, Queen of Scots* (1895), *Nero and the Burning of Rome* (1908), and *The Last Days of Pompeii* (1908) provided early, primitive versions of what would eventually become some of the other subgenres of historical cinema, embryonic versions of the topical film and the epic. The first films to capture the spectacular power of the cinema to re-create the past, however, were epic films made in Italy between 1910 and 1914. They were also the first to extend the screening time of films to two and three hours or more. Epic works such as *Quo Vadis?* (1912), *Cabiria* (1914), and *Spartacus* (1913) were vast, sweeping depictions of the ancient world that united spectacle, lavish set design, and narrative in a way that had an enormous influence on film style, and that brought an extraordinary amount of publicity to the films even before their release. The Italian epics of the early silent period provided a particular incentive to D.W. Griffith, who after seeing *Quo Vadis?* in 1913 decided to make a two-reel biblical film, *Judith of Bethulia* (1914). The grandest of the Italian epics, *Cabiria*, by Giovanni Pastrone, commanded so much public attention for its length, epic form, and massive sets that just hearing about it prompted Griffith to begin planning his own epic, *The Birth of a Nation* (1915). And after actually seeing *Cabiria*, according to Robert Sklar, Griffith began planning an even larger-scale narrative that would interweave four historical periods, a film that would result in the ambitious *Intolerance*, released in 1916.[8]

The Birth of a Nation is generally credited with inaugurating the genre of the historical film in the United States. Although films that used historical settings and included historical characters were fairly common by 1915, they could not be considered serious attempts to understand or explain the past: rather, they consisted of romances, costume dramas, tales of adventure, or small historical vignettes set within larger dramatic narratives, such as a scene in *Uncle Tom's Cabin* (1903) with Little Eva looking down from heaven on the divisive events of American history. *The Birth of a Nation*, on the other hand, attempts to offer an explanation and interpretation of the most troubled and damaging period in US history; despite its offensive stereotypes and obvious racism, it poses serious questions and makes serious interpretations about the meaning of the past.[9]

The Birth of a Nation sets forth a highly controversial thesis about the nation's past and future, and the causes and consequences of large-scale historical events – the Civil War and Reconstruction. In its ambitiousness, its notoriety, and its insistence on presenting a serious, if deeply flawed, interpretation about the meaning of the past, *The Birth of a Nation* brings into relief the distinctive characteristics of the genre and provides a blueprint for the future development of the historical film. It melds an elaborate family romance with a story of national trauma and national reconciliation; it employs a visual vocabulary consisting of wide panoramic shots, elaborate cross-cutting, and the use of close-ups as a form of historical commentary and analysis; and it insists upon the authenticity of its representations by closely imitating battlefield daguerreotypes, by asserting the authenticity of its depiction of the assassination of Abraham Lincoln, and by dwelling on the lived spaces of the historical past, the porches, picket fences, and dirt roads of the South.

Yet for all its bigotry and offensive stereotyping, the film accurately reflected the prevailing historical understanding and knowledge of the era in which it was produced. Although it was challenged at the time, its depiction of Reconstruction matched the beliefs of the most powerful school of American historians of that era, including President Woodrow Wilson, the former head of the American Historical Society, who, after a private screening, purportedly commented: "It's like writing history with Lightning. And my only regret is that it is all so terribly true."[10]

Partly in response to the negative publicity Griffith received with *The Birth of a Nation*, he produced an even more ambitious film, *Intolerance*,

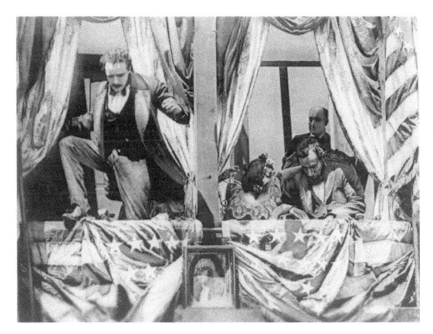

FIGURE 1.1 "Sic semper tyrannus!" Reenactment as facsimile: John Wilkes Booth (Raoul Walsh) leaping from the balcony after assassinating Abraham Lincoln (Joseph Henabery) in D. W. Griffith's *The Birth of a Nation* (1915) [Joseph Brenner Associates Inc./Photofest]

in 1916. This massive work combines four stories set in different time periods, and interweaves them in a complex arrangement, like a musical fugue. The thematic link among these stories was the idea of intolerance through the ages and the overcoming of it through love. By cutting these four stories together through parallel editing – which up to that time had been used strictly for cutting between parallel actions in the same time frame – Griffith attempted to articulate a universal historical patterning, one that linked the story of Christ's crucifixion with a modern story of injustice, the fall of ancient Babylon, and the story of the St. Bartholomew Day Massacre in sixteenth-century France. This innovative use of parallel editing to link and harmonize four separate historical narratives was a dazzling conceptual breakthrough, but it was not well received by the public, and *Intolerance* was a commercial failure. The artist who had accustomed audiences to a certain style of cinematic discourse contradicted his own proven model and fashioned a work that was experimental, formally complex, and driven by ideas.

FIGURE 1.2 Outside the Babylon Gate, one of the magnificent sets of D. W. Griffith's *Intolerance* (1916) [Photofest]

Griffith's Influence

Nevertheless, *Intolerance* had a widespread impact on later filmmakers, particularly the Soviet filmmakers Sergei Eisenstein and Vledesov Pudovkin, and also on the work of French filmmaker Abel Gance, who used many of Griffith's ideas in *Napoleon* (1927).

Griffith's influence in creating a cinematic style of historical narration is perhaps best seen in the Soviet cinema of the 1920s. Eisenstein expanded on Griffith's formal innovations in editing to create an even more advanced visual aesthetic known as montage editing, a style characterized by rapid, dynamic combinations of shots of very short length. Eisenstein used this style to create a history, or better, a foundational mythology for the fledgling Soviet Union. In *Potemkin* (1925), Eisenstein takes a small-scale historical incident – the mutiny of a small group of sailors on board the battleship *Potemkin* during the czarist period – and turned it into a stirring dramatization of the power of the proletariat to overcome oppression and create a revolution. In *October* (1927), also known as *Ten Days That Shook the World*, Eisenstein followed the turbulent events of the ten days of the Bolshevik revolution. The film combines close attention to the actual events with an elaborate set of visual ideas including the use of visual metaphors, repetition, humor, and a highly charged sense of movement and dynamism.

The Soviet filmmakers were experimental in their treatment of the historical past, exploring ways of creating a revolutionary historiography for a revolutionary time. The style of historical narration that they pioneered had an impact on the Latin American cinema of the 1960s and, more recently, on Oliver Stone's *JFK* (1991) and *Nixon* (1995).

The War Film

The war film is one of the great modes of cinematic expression, with outstanding examples of the subgenre stretching from the silent period to the contemporary era. It includes such formidable Hollywood productions such as *All Quiet on the Western Front* (1930), *Hell's Angels* (1930), *The Big Parade* (1925), *The Charge of the Light Brigade* (1936), *The Longest Day* (1962), *Tora, Tora, Tora* (1970), *Glory* (1989), *Saving Private Ryan* (1999), *The Thin Red Line* (1999), *Flags of Our Fathers* (2006), and *Letters from Iwo Jima* (2007). The earliest war films coincide with the beginnings of the cinema itself. Widespread enthusiasm for rewitnessing war on film motivated people to rush to the vaudeville houses and other sites where films were shown to see images of the troops, the battleships, and staged battle scenes.

These very early films can be can be grouped into three main types that together comprise the major conventions of the subgenre: the documenting of events connected to the war, such as the Edison film, *The Burial of the "Maine" Victims*; reenactments of major battles, such as *U.S. Infantry Supported by Rough Riders at El Caney*, and short narrative films that combine battle sequences, scenes of life in the camp, and images of life on the home front, such as *Love and War*.[11] Films such as these were extremely abbreviated, lasting only a minute or two in length, but they can be seen as rough sketches of the war film in its full development. In some cases, scenes reenacting combat were juxtaposed with sequences set at the home front, or representing the give and take of life in the camp "behind the lines." Battle, the camaraderie and horseplay of the soldiers, the families at home, the funeral and the homecoming, can be found in the earliest war films, and have remained standard throughout the history of the form.

Many war films have been applauded for their realism and for their focus on the cruelties of war, as well as for their portraits of heroism.

The authenticity of the war film, however, often considered its most outstanding feature, is achieved in almost every case through extraordinary artifice. D. W. Griffith, for example, was severely disappointed with the reality of the battlefield when he was granted access to the front during World War I to film *Hearts of the World* (1918). The monotony of trench warfare, and the lack of drama in the protracted battles or sieges where soldiers went for months without even seeing the enemy, was not what he had envisioned the struggle of men and armies would actually look like. The documentaries coming from the front were equally drab, consisting mostly of exercises, military parades, and the aftermath of battle. The actual battlefield was far too dangerous for the cameraman, and the bulkiness and weight of film equipment made it impossible to document actual hostilities. Griffith found that combat scenes could only be fashioned in the studio.

The war film achieved both critical and popular success with *The Big Parade* (1925), *Hell's Angels* (1930), *Wings* (1927), *The Dawn Patrol* (1930), and *All Quiet on the Western Front* (1930). *The Big Parade*, directed by King Vidor and released in 1925, became the model for many subsequent films of ground combat. The film's centerpiece is its battle sequences, especially a night battle scene that captures the nightmarish aspect of war on the Western Front. *Hell's Angels*, directed and produced at great expense by Howard Hughes, captured the extraordinary excitement of aerial combat. Hughes purchased and equipped his own squadron of World War I-era fighter planes, and filmed the dogfight sequences with an eye to verisimilitude. The extraordinary authenticity of the aerial combat, filmed entirely in live action sequences, compares with the most accomplished work of much later films. Moreover, the heartbreaking scenes aboard a German zeppelin, and the more intimate moments of human connection between the two brothers who serve as the main characters, provide a counterpoint to the excitement of the spectacle of air battle, emphasizing the human dimension of war and the poignancy of loss and sacrifice that it demands.

Lewis Milestone's *All Quiet on the Western Front*, which won Oscars for Best Picture and Best Director in 1930, received international and popular acclaim for its portrait of the horrors of war as experienced by a young German soldier. *All Quiet on the Western Front* established not only the power and commercial viability of the war film, but also established the Great War as an enduring emblem of human loss. Although war is one of the subjects that helps define the genre of the historical film, *All Quiet on the Western Front* articulated the antiwar sentiment that is so often a theme of these films: it posed serious questions about the

FIGURE 1.3 Carnage in the trenches: the war film as antiwar drama in Lewis Milestone's *All Quiet on the Western Front* (1930) [Universal Pictures/Photofest]

consequences of nationalism and patriotism, and stressed the dehumanizing effects of war, themes that would be taken up in later films such as *Paths of Glory* (1957), *Born on the Fourth of July* (1989), and *Apocalypse Now* (1979). The film is also unique for showing the effects of war from the perspective of a young German soldier, the first time Germans were treated sympathetically in Hollywood films made after the war. On the technical and artistic level, the film broke new ground with its use of elaborate, moving camera shots, created by using a mobile crane in the battle scenes – the most extensive use of moving camera in a sound film up to that time.

The Longest Day (1962), produced by Darryl F. Zanuck, is often considered the most towering achievement of the war film subgenre. Zanuck called it the "most ambitious undertaking since *Gone with the Wind* and *The Birth of a Nation*" when he announced it in 1960.[12] It inaugurated a trend toward combat spectaculars in the historical film genre, a trend that extends to the present. The combination of extraordinary realism in the battle scenes and exceptional attentiveness to the small dramas unfolding among the individual soldiers provided the model for many films to come, among them *Saving Private Ryan* and *Letters from Iwo Jima*. The film also set a new standard for authenticity in the historical genre, in some scenes replicating the Normandy invasion so closely that stills taken from the shooting of the film and stills taken from the actual invasion are almost indistinguishable. Moving away from the one-sided patriotism of earlier films dealing with World War II, the film depicts the German soldiers in a somewhat sympathetic light. *The Longest Day* solidified the importance of the historical film in the second half of the twentieth century, and drew a worldwide audience to its treatment of the Allied effort. It successfully merged a documentary approach to historical filmmaking with the needs of commercial drama.

In the late 1970s, the American cinema began to take on the subject of Vietnam. Francis Ford Coppola's *Apocalypse Now* was released in 1979, and along with Michael Cimino's 1978 *The Deer Hunter*, films began portraying the war as a pathological endeavor that suggested the ruin of a generation of young Americans. Moreover, both the budget and production problems associated with these films seemed to mirror the self-destructive nature of the subject of the Vietnam War. Although both films had moments of exceptional cinematic grandeur, they became as well known for their outsized budgets and on-set turmoil as for their messages about the self-destruction and insanity of war. It was not until 1986, with the release of Oliver Stone's *Platoon*, that the Vietnam subgenre began to flourish as a dominant mode of cinematic expression. Stone followed *Platoon* with the magisterial *Born on the Fourth of July* (1989), a powerful and moving antiwar film that dealt with the trauma of the returning Vietnam veteran. A sober and scathingly critical work, *Born on the Fourth of July* followed in the tradition of *The Best Years of Our Lives* (1946) in illustrating the profound alienation of returning veterans who have been traumatized by the experience of war.

The traditional war film experienced a resurgence at the turn of the century with films such as *Saving Private Ryan, Black Hawk Down* (2001), *Glory, Pearl Harbor* (2001), and *The Patriot* (2000) reestablishing the power and appeal of films that crystallize the heroism and sacrifice that war entails. *Saving Private Ryan* is an especially good example. Celebrated for the authenticity of its battlefield sequences as well as for its powerful evocation of nostalgia for the certainties of the "last good war," the film resurrected the traditional war film, which had fallen into disrepute in the post-Vietnam period, and reestablished it as a dominant form in American cinema. In rehearsing and reinvigorating the genre motifs and conventions of the war films of the past, however,

Saving Private Ryan also broke new ground in its technological innovations. Much of its success was based on its special effects, most powerfully displayed in the Omaha Beach landing sequence, in which the film blends computer-generated imagery, live action photography, reenactments of documentary photographs and sequences, accelerated editing, slow-motion cinematography, and electronically enhanced sound design. *Saving Private Ryan* combines the traditions of the war film – stressing the importance of the individual soldier and the success of the collective endeavor mounted on his behalf – with advanced visual and acoustic techniques that give it a powerful claim to authenticity. It became the defining expression of the culture of commemoration that has developed around the achievements of the veterans of World War II.

Quite different in tone and message, *Flags of Our Fathers* and *Letters from Iwo Jima* explore the culminating battle in the Pacific during World War II and emphasize the vast gulf between the images of war promoted by the media, including the cinema, and experiences "on the ground." The two films, both directed by Clint Eastwood, are the first war films to tell both sides of the story in a full-length and fully considered fashion. *Flags of Our Fathers* focuses on the American experience during the Battle of Iwo Jima and the subsequent media campaign the US government developed around the iconic image of the American flag being raised over the island. The soldiers involved in the flag-raising were celebrated in US media culture, and were immediately pressed into service to perform reenactments throughout the United States for the purpose of raising war bonds. As the reenactments unfold, each of the four soldiers remembers the actual events that occurred, memories that foreground the difference between the public relations campaign and the reality of the battle, and each experiences a crisis of conscience. *Letters from Iwo Jima*, which was released soon after *Flags of Our Fathers*, presents the story of the battle of Iwo Jima from the Japanese perspective, rendering the extraordinarily harsh experience of the Japanese soldiers defending their homeland during the attack. The human story of the Japanese general commanding the island, whose letters and drawings to his son and wife were buried in a cave and not discovered until 1996, provide the rhetorical frame for the story. The events play out from the perspective of the general, the enlisted men, and the lower-ranking officers, with the dialogue almost entirely in Japanese. And the ostensibly iconic moment of the first film, the raising of the flag, is registered in *Letters from Iwo Jima* as barely visible, a small speck on a hilltop, signifying to the Japanese merely that a certain position had been overtaken. The two films together, although quite different in terms of style and approach, provide a powerful and heartbreaking portrayal of the catastrophic consequences of war to those fighting it, even to the victor.

The Epic Film

Many of the most important filmmakers in world cinema have created epic films, including D.W. Griffith, Cecil B. DeMille, William Wyler, Anthony Mann, Sergei Eisenstein, Stanley Kubrick, and Akira Kurosawa. As Derek Elley writes, "The epic genre has seen some of the cinema's greatest stylists and craftsmen working at full stretch, several spending their formative years associated with historical films."[13] The Italian film-maker Enrico Guazzoni inaugurated the form with *Quo Vadis?* in 1912, a story of the legend and martyrdom of St. Peter. An early version of the Spartacus story, *Spataco* (1913), by Ernesto Pasquale, soon followed. With the world success of Giovanni Pastrone's *Cabiria* in 1914, the elements of epic cinema were established. A vast, sweeping work of monumental sets and massed crowd scenes, featuring a romance between a slave girl and a Roman centurion, *Cabiria* was the first true screen epic. It was quickly followed in Italy by many films dealing with ancient Rome, Greece, and early Christianity.

Following the worldwide success of the Italian spectacle films, which were widely regarded as the finest achievements of the early silent cinema, Griffith released *The Birth of a Nation*, a film that established the viability of longer, ambitious historical films for the American cinema. And driven to produce a film of even greater scope by a desire to compete with the monumental *Cabiria*, Griffith expanded on his earlier biblical film, *Judith of Bethulia*, to create *Intolerance* (1916), which remains today one of the most ambitious films ever made. *Intolerance* did not meet with commercial or critical approval, however, and the production of epic films in America lapsed. In the early 1920s, the epic form was half-heartedly revived in DeMille's *The Ten Commandments* (1923) and Alexander Korda's *Samson and Delilah* (1923), both of which were only partially set in the ancient past.

In 1925, *Ben-Hur: A Tale of the Christ*, directed by Fred Niblo, was released by MGM. Building on the enormous success of the stage production and the continuing success of the novel by General Lew Wallace – apart from the Bible, the novel had been the bestselling book in America for many decades – *Ben-Hur: A Tale of the Christ* became a commercial blockbuster. Featuring stunning color sequences, a chariot race that remains one of the greatest action sequences ever filmed, and

FIGURE 1.4 Judah Ben-Hur (Ramon Novarro) driving the chariot in a scene that defined the American epic on stage and on screen (1925) [MGM/Photofest]

exceptional treatments of the set pieces that made the play the most successful theatrical production in history, *Ben-Hur* was a magisterial accomplishment, consolidating the reputation of Hollywood as the primary producer of epic films.

In the 1930s, films such as *The Sign of the Cross* (1933), *Cleopatra* (1934), and *The Last Days of Pompeii* (1935) drew enormous crowds. *The Sign of the Cross* also created a good deal of controversy for its depictions of "pagan" sexuality and the extreme violence and sensationalism of scenes set in the arena. Its message of Christian uplift notwithstanding, the film was largely responsible for the institution of the Hayes Code, the censorship formula adopted by the studios in order to placate conservative critics. DeMille produced the more restrained *Cleopatra* the following year, and demonstrated that suggestiveness and indirection could be as effective as blatant sensationalism in conveying the ancient milieu. *The Sign of the Cross* was reissued during World War II, with a prologue and coda added. The new release featured a Catholic, Protestant, and Jewish chaplain in an airplane approaching Rome as part of a bombing run.

Here, the Allied liberation of Italy was compared with the liberation of pagan Rome by early Christianity, as the fires from the bombs dissolve into the burning by Nero of the ancient capitol that inaugurates the film. A film that had been widely criticized for its overt and sensational displays of sex and violence was converted to a message of liberation and American virtue on its re-release during wartime.

In the mid- to late 1930s through the 1940s, however, the epic form waned as audience's tastes turned to contemporary subjects, exemplified in the sophisticated musicals and comedies of Hollywood, and in the later development of realism, exemplified by the rise of serious dramas and the ascendance of the psychological thriller. But the form returned full force in the early 1950s, with *Quo Vadis* (1951), directed by Mervyn LeRoy, and *The Robe* (1953), directed by Henry Koster, the first film to be shot in CinemaScope. The epic, with its lavish sets and mass choreography of crowds and armies, lent itself to the widescreen format that was one of Hollywood's responses to the threat of television.

DeMille's *The Ten Commandments* (1956) marked a return to the subject he had first treated in 1923. Perhaps more than any other film, *The Ten Commandments* embodies the historiographic vision of the Hollywood epic, which the theorist Gilles Deleuze defines as an overlay of three different ways of depicting the past: the monumental, the antiquarian, and the critical-ethical. In its dazzling portrayal of ancient Egypt, especially in its enormous sets and its massed crowd scenes, the film exemplifies the monumental vision of the past. In its use of color, especially in the concentrated attention to fabrics, jewelry, and ornamentation, the film renders an antiquarian perspective on the past. And in its spectacular scenes of the green, snaking fog descending from on high to fell the first-born of Egypt, the parting of the Red Sea, and the exodus from Egypt, the film expresses an unambiguous critical-ethical message linking religion and popular liberation. In 1956, it was also seen as an expression of American virtue in the threatening political environment of the Cold War, a statement against totalitarian regimes past and present. In the closing shot of the film, Moses, played by Charlton Heston, stands on an outcrop of Mount Sinai, his right hand raised in farewell, his left hand clasped across his chest, emulating the pose of the Statue of Liberty. The American epic, Deleuze writes, "communicates via the peaks" with the great civilizations of the past. *The Ten Commandments* has been re-released several times since its initial 1956 run, and remains today a staple of television programming, especially on major holidays.

In 1959, William Wyler directed *Ben-Hur*, a film that for most critics represents the high point of the style. Wyler had been an assistant on

FIGURE 1.5 Ben-Hur (Charlton Heston) and Messala (Stephen Boyd) in *Ben-Hur*, considered by many to be the highest achievement of the epic form (1959) [Metro-Goldwyn-Mayer/Photofest]

the set of the 1925 *Ben-Hur*, and quotes the earlier film in a number of sequences, including the famous chariot race, which has numerous shots taken directly from the original. Among its many outstanding accomplishments, the score by Miklós Rózsa is widely considered to be one of the finest works of music written for film. The overall progress of the film, which moves from Judea to Rome and back, depicts two great civilizations in conflict. But rather than rehearsing the traditional epic themes – the emergence of a people or the fulfillment of a heroic destiny – *Ben-Hur* culminates in an act of forgiveness, a theme that is expressed throughout the film in the simple symbolism of water, which, at the end, floods the courtyard of Ben-Hur's home.

King of Kings, directed by Nicolas Ray, and *El Cid*, directed by Anthony Mann, both released in 1961, were also accomplished works. *El Cid*, a medieval epic, depicts the story of the Cid, the Spanish national hero who united the Christians and the Moors in Spain against the conquest of a radical Islamist sect from Morocco, the Almoravid. Loosely based on the Spanish national epic poem, the *Poema de Mio Cid*, the film is a compelling work that in today's political context seems remarkably prescient. Produced by Samuel Bronston in Spain, the film strove to be received as an international production, with stars from America (Charlton Heston), France (Geneviève Page), and Italy (Sophia Loren). With a score by Miklós Rósza, the film has an epic grandeur that is stately, poetic, and moving.

The epic form in Hollywood reached its zenith in the early 1960s with *Cleopatra* (1963), directed by Joseph L. Mankiewicz, *The Fall of the Roman Empire* (1964), directed by Anthony Mann, and *Spartacus* (1960), directed by Stanley Kubrick. An impressive work, *Spartacus* became famous upon its release for the fact that it credited as screenwriter Dalton Trumbo, a prominent leftist who had been blacklisted in Hollywood for refusing to cooperate with the House Un-American Activities Committee. *Spartacus* became known as "the film that broke the blacklist." Partly because of expense and partly because of extraordinary off-screen publicity, *Cleopatra* also became notorious for its production circumstances, namely the romance of its two stars, Elizabeth Taylor and Richard Burton, factors that had nothing to do with the exceptional quality of the film. Although three of the top five grossing films in Hollywood during the 1950s were epics – *The Robe*, *The Ten Commandments*, and *Ben-Hur*, the cultural mood in the 1960s had begun to shift.

The epic form went into sudden eclipse with *The Fall of the Roman Empire*, a film that was critically well received but did not connect at the box office. From 1964 until recent years, the epic was decidedly out of fashion. With the release of *Braveheart* (1995), directed by Mel Gibson, and *Gladiator* (2000), by Ridley Scott, the epic has renewed itself in a way that heralds a return to cultural prominence. *Gladiator*, in particular, provides a fascinating example of the use of new visual technologies to narrate the Roman past. Its use of computer-generated imagery to re-create the Colosseum and the Roman Forum gives the film a spectacular visual style that updates and goes beyond the monumental style of earlier epic films, equaling in visual excitement the accomplishments of *The Ten Commandments* and *Ben-Hur*. Like *El Cid*, *Gladiator* was produced and marketed as an international production, and enjoyed enormous world success. Following the success of *Gladiator*, several new epic films have been released, including *Troy* (2004), directed by Wolfgang Petersen, *Alexander* (2004), directed by Oliver Stone, and *Kingdom of Heaven* (2005), also directed by Ridley Scott.

One of the leading scholars of epic film, Derek Elley, maintains that the epic form requires a certain temporal distance from the period being portrayed; the quality of mythic grandeur that we associate with the epic, he feels, can only be fully expressed in works that deal with the remote past. He sets the outer historical limit of the epic at the early medieval period, arguing "It is the peculiar ability of the epic to derive its basis from very real events but to transmute the ingredients into a timeless form; the past has always excited man's imagination more than the tangible present, since it gives him greater scope to dream." To support this point, Elley draws on the description of the epic, given by Aristotle in his *On the Art of Poetry*: "it is clear . . . that the [epic] poet's job is not to say what happened but what *could* happen."[14] Historical periods that are too close to the present, in Elley's view, restrict the timeless, mythic qualities that distinguish epic form.

Many critics would regard Elley's requirement of historical distance as too limiting. It eliminates a great many films that seem to possess the requisite epic grandeur and scale of epic cinema, films such as Francis Ford Coppola's *The Godfather, Parts I and II* (1972, 1974), Bernardo Bertolucci's *1900* (1977), and Martin Scorsese's *Gangs of New York* (2003). These films create a powerful impression of a historical world and a historical milieu, although actual historical events are only incidental to their plots. Here, the traditional epic themes – the founding of a people or nation, the advent of freedom, the fulfillment of a heroic destiny – are expressed in terms of generational struggles and the rising and falling arc of a long family history. These films form a subset of the epic film, the family epic, a type that accents certain features of the epic while others recede into the background. The critical-ethical perspective that Deleuze finds to be essential to the epic form manifests itself throughout these works. The monumental and antiquarian characteristics of epic style, however, are largely missing from the family epic.

The Biographical Film

Despite its small-bore critical reputation, the biographical film has a long and distinguished history in world cinema. In addition to its surprising and enduring popularity – more biographical films have been produced than any other type of historical film – it has often advanced the fortunes of entire national cinemas. *The Private Life of Henry VIII* (1933), directed by Alexander Korda, for example, was the British cinema's first international success, and Charles Laughton won an Oscar for Best Actor for his portrayal of the monarch. Abel Gance's *Napoleon* (1927) brought a similar sense of national pride to France, a country whose film industry had been devastated by World War I. Still regarded as one of the most outstanding achievements in the history of the cinema, *Napoleon* was seen as the culmination of the French cinema's rise from near-annihilation in 1914. Sergei Eisenstein's *Ivan the Terrible* (1944) was produced with the specific intention of rallying the Soviet people and troops to the effort required for World War II. And more recently, Bernardo Bertolucci's *The Last Emperor* (1987), the story of a character who started life as the Emperor of China and ended under Mao's rule as a humble gardener, won nine Academy Awards and claimed the historical significance of being the first film to be shot on location in Beijing's Forbidden City, heralding a more open era in Chinese–Western cultural relations.

Nevertheless, the biographical film suffers from a lack of critical respect. Roland Barthes has called biography "the fiction that dare not speak its name," and the biographical film, apart from a few works that have achieved worldwide success, has often been taken as a kind of critical embarrassment.[15] It is widely regarded as a lesser cultural form, a mainstream entertainment that creates mythic figures out of complex human beings. Its style of historiography is also regarded as suspect, a dubious attempt to encapsulate or exemplify a major historical period in the life of an individual protagonist.

Further appraisal of the form, however, reveals the biographical film to be part of a deep cultural tradition of depicting exemplary lives for the purpose of ethical instruction, a tradition that dates back at least to the medieval period. Leo Lowenthal, an influential member of the Frankfurt School, described biography as a continuation of the forms of instruction found in the "Lives of the Saints." As one writer explains, "Lowenthal felt that biographies . . . helped prepare average people to accept their place in the social structure by valorizing a common, distant, and elevated set of lives that readers could hope to emulate."[16] The form taken by this tradition in the 1940s, however, revealed to Lowenthal a drastic decline in American culture. Analyzing popular magazines, which often featured biographies of famous Americans, he discovered a substantial shift: where American biography of the early twentieth century focused on industrial leaders, such as Henry Ford and Thomas Edison, and emphasized effort and achievement, contemporary biography privileged movie stars and celebrities, icons of glamour and consumption. The public celebrity that defined success in American culture, in Lowenthal's view, illuminated the pervasive and negative effects of the "culture industry," which promoted acquisition over achievement, consumption over effort.[17]

Although Lowenthal had a negative view of American culture, his recognition of the importance of biography as a form of cultural expression is borne out by the success and the influence of the biographical film. It emerged as a recognizable Hollywood subgenre in the 1930s, with films that focused on humanitarian and political figures. The first major biographical film is generally considered to be *Disraeli* (1929), a film starring George Arliss and marketed as a Warner Bros. prestige production. Arliss won an Academy Award for Best Actor for his portrayal. In 1931, he starred in *Alexander Hamilton* for Warner Bros., and in 1933 he continued his success in these films with *Voltaire*. The commercial and critical accomplishment of these works paved the way for several later Warner Bros. films directed by William Dieterle, including *The Life of Louis Pasteur* (1936), for which Paul Muni won the Oscar for Best Actor; *White Angel* (1936), a story of Florence Nightingale; *The Life of Emile Zola* (1937); and *Juarez* (1939), both also starring Muni. Darryl F. Zanuck recognized the strength of the biographical film, and when he left Warner Bros. in 1933 to found Twentieth Century Pictures, he immediately began making films with George Arliss such as *The House of Rothschild* (1934) and *Cardinal Richelieu* (1935).

The heroic tradition established in the Warner Bros. films was advanced by movies depicting the early life of Abraham Lincoln in the late 1930s. John Ford's *Young Mr. Lincoln* (1939), starring Henry Fonda in his first film with Ford, and *Abe Lincoln in Illinois*, starring Raymond Massey, were not so much historical as mythological exercises, as neither film was particularly accurate with regard to the actual events of Lincoln's life, nor to his character. Nevertheless, *Young Mr. Lincoln*, in particular, succeeded in elevating Lincoln's early years to the level of national myth, reinforcing the widespread cult of Lincoln that had developed in the mid- to late 1930s, exemplified by Carl Sandburg's popular biographies.[18]

Biographical films are often driven by a national, myth-making impulse, but as the subgenre matured, complex portraits that revealed the darker impulses of character became more prominent. Outside of the American cinema, Sergei Eisenstein's *Ivan the Terrible* (1945), for example, focused on an individual protagonist, rather than the collective protagonist of his earlier films, in part in order to rally the Soviet people during World War II by giving them a biographical hero who had unified Russia, fought off treachery, and defeated external enemies in the sixteenth century. But it may also be the first biographical film to explore the darker side of its main character, depicting Ivan, especially in Part II, as driven by revenge. He presides over mass executions, tortures, and murderous intrigue, and turns into a cruel dictator, a monstrous figure, a portrayal that led to the film being banned by Stalin in 1946. As David Bordwell writes in his magisterial study of Eisenstein, "Surrounded by enemies and traitors, increasingly isolated from family and friends, Ivan ruthlessly pursues his goal. Yet the closer he comes to achieving it, the more empty of human contact his life becomes."[19]

The shift in biographical films to more complex portraits is exemplified by the powerful portrayal of T. S. Lawrence, another biography made outside Hollywood. *Lawrence of Arabia* (1962), starring Peter O'Toole, paints an arresting portrait of its main character that shows him as both heroic and fatally flawed. The Hollywood biopic took a similar multidimensional approach with *Patton* (1970), in which George C. Scott depicts the notorious World War II cavalry general as both a noble warrior and a vainglorious egomaniac. The complex and subtle shadings of character that distinguish films such as *Lawrence of Arabia* and *Patton* are also found in more recent examples of the form. The important and innovative *Reds* (1982) by Warren Beatty – the story of the left-wing journalist John Reed, one of the few Westerners buried in the Kremlin, also exemplify this tendency. Works such as *The Last Emperor* (1987) by Bernardo Bertolucci and Oliver Stone's *Nixon* (1995) are distinguished examples of works that take a complicated view of the link between the individual subject and the historical process, refusing to see the individual agent as simply the crystallized expression of historical forces. *Schindler's List* (1995), directed by Steven Spielberg, *Malcolm X* (1993), directed by Spike Lee, *Gandhi* (1982), directed by Richard Attenborough, and *Aviator* (2005), directed by Martin Scorsese are also fine examples of films that consider the question that is at the heart of the biographical film – the relationship between the currents and forces of history and the charismatic individual who strives to shape those forces.

The cultural shift to cults of celebrity that Lowenthal noticed in the rise of fan magazines in the 1940s seems not to be the case with the Hollywood biopic, which even in its most popular forms centers on the lives of figures whose confrontation with celebrity is often their undoing. The musical biopic, perhaps the most successful variant of the form, has provided powerful and sobering portrayals of figures as diverse as Benny Goodman, Cole Porter, Jim Morrison, Buddy Holly, Richie Valens, Ludwig von Beethoven, Frederic Chopin, and Amadeus Mozart. Recent musical biopics have been enormously successful, winning numerous awards and drawing large audiences. *Ray* (2004), directed by Taylor Hackford, renders the story of Ray Charles in a form that emphasizes his overcoming of extraordinary adversity, including childhood blindness, guilt from the accidental death of his younger brother, racism, and drugs. In *Walk the Line* (2005), a powerful portrayal of the singer Johnny Cash, the early history of rock and roll is vividly portrayed. Here, the redemption of the character from drugs and self-loathing is folded into the story of Cash's famous climb-any-mountain love affair with June Carter. In the musical biopic form, the dramatic arc is redemptive; in contrast to the tragic denouement that is so powerfully expressed in films such as *Patton*, *Lawrence of Arabia*, and *Nixon*; the musical biopic is most often resolved in scenes of reconciliation and acceptance. Where a tragic ending occurs, it comes not from the characters' own flaws, but rather from accident, almost as if fate had intervened, as in the plane crash that ends the lives of Buddy Holly and Richie Valens, and the illness that leads to the early death of Amadeus Mozart.

The Topical Film

Many important historical films center on a particular incident or focus on a specific period rather than on the grand narratives of war, the fulfillment of a heroic destiny, or the emergence of a people or a nation. Films that deal with a specific event may be called topical films, as exemplified by such celebrated works as Rossellini's *Rome, Open City* (1945), and *Paisan* (1946), Jean Renoir's *La Marseillaise* (1938), Andrez Wajda's *Danton* (1982), *Eight Men Out* (1988) and *Matewan* (1987), both directed by John Sayles, Peter Weir's *Gallipoli* (1981), and James Cameron's *Titanic* (1999). The most recent examples of important topical films are *United 93* (2006), directed by Paul Greengrass, and *World Trade Center* (2006), directed by Oliver Stone.

Independent filmmaker John Sayles has provided a capsule definition of the topical film:

> Am I going to recreate this entire historical world, or am I going to take one episode that stands for it? In making *Matewan* I chose to focus on the Matewan Massacre because it seemed to me that this episode epitomized a fifteen-year period of American labor history. To make it even more representative, I incorporated things that weren't literally true of the Matewan Massacre – such as the percentage of miners who were black – but were true of that general fifteen-year period.[20]

Similarly, Sayles's *Eight Men Out*, a film that focuses on the Black Sox scandal of 1919 in which several players conspired to throw the World Series, dug under the surface of the incident to show the period as a moment of cultural transition in which sports, advertising, public relations, gambling, leisure, and mass communications were beginning to transform the nation from an agrarian culture to an urban, commodity-based society.

Other historical films are important not for the specific events that they portray, but for their exactitude of period detail and for their attempt to render the social codes of the past, what Collingwood might call the "inside of the historical event."[21] A kind of shorthand phrase – period films – has been used to describe this type, which in general are characterized by their attempt to express fully a cultural order that is remote and is organized according to different allegiances and beliefs. Examples include *The Return of Martin Guerre* (1981), by Daniel Vigne, *Black Robe* (1991), by Bruce Beresford, *Daughters of the Dust* (1991), by Julie Dash, and *Gangs of New York* (2003), by Martin Scorsese.

Black Robe, a particularly fine example of a period film, centers on the challenges facing Jesuit missionaries in French Canada in the 1600s. The story revolves around the attempt by one young priest to travel to a distressed mission in the Ottawa River valley, a journey that becomes an ordeal. The film captures the strangeness and sense of otherness that the priest experiences while traveling among the Algonquin band that serve as his trading partners and guides, but it also gives us the perspective of the Indians and effectively opens a window onto their cultural sensibility. The priest, Father Laforgue, is as strange and incomprehensible to the Indians as they are to him, with his black robes, his lack of interest in women and pelts, his ability to read minds at a distance (which is how they interpret his ability to read), and what seems to them odd behavior, as when he tries to baptize a dead Indian child, an act that the Indians interpret as a curse. Each culture is presented to the viewer in its unfiltered strangeness, much as it must have seemed to the Algonquins, on the one hand, and the Jesuit missionaries, on the other, in 1634.

Martin Scorsese has said that *Gangs of New York* is not based on actual historical events: "the film isn't based on facts in the way that, let's say, *Glory* is . . . History is suggested and there's the impression of a world."[22] The film portrays a little-known period in American history, beginning in 1846 and ending in the early 1860s with the draft riots in New York City. Bitter conflicts between the native-born residents of the slums and the multiple waves of Irish immigrants entering New York to escape famine provide the historical context for the story. The film begins with a bloody tribal battle between two slum gangs, the "Native Americans" and the "Dead Rabbits," who have allies among other Irish gangs such as the "Pug Uglies" and the "Forty Thieves." When the leader of the Dead Rabbits, Priest Vallon, is killed in the battle, the film develops into a classic revenge tale, as the young Amsterdam Vallon, the son of the slain leader, seeks to avenge his death at the hands of "Bill the Butcher." The psychological tension between the two, which one character in the film calls "Shakespearian," complicates the story. It is the portrayal of the notorious "Five Points" neighborhood in Manhattan, however, described by one writer as the "world's worst slum," that distinguishes Scorsese's film. It immerses the viewer in a spectacularly squalid and primitive world whose epicenter is the "Old Brewery" building situated in the Five Points. Scorsese built an enormous set at the Cinecittà studios in Rome, and rendered the style of the era with exceptional vividness, bringing to life the description given by the Revd. Matthew Hale Smith in the 1840s of the Five Points: "it is a region of wickedness, filth, and woe. Lodging-houses are under ground, foul and slimy, without ventilation, and often without windows, and overrun with rats and every species of vermin . . . Children are born in sorrow, and raised in reeking vice and bestiality, that no heathen degradation can exceed."[23] Although the film is loosely populated with actual historical figures, such as "Boss" Tweed and Horace Greeley, the main focus of the film is the portrayal of the milieu – the setting of the Five Points, the codes of honor that characterize the various gangs that vie for dominance, such as the "Native Americans" and the "Dead Rabbits," and the volatile mixture of different populations – Chinese, Irish, African, and Anglo-American – that fill the dance halls and saloons. In rendering this explosive period setting, *Gangs of New York* fulfills the dictum laid down by Natalie Zemon Davis for historical films to "let the past be the past."[24]

United 93 and *World Trade Center* are primary examples of the topical film, works that focus on a singular historical event. Each film portrays the events of 9/11 in a deliberately circumscribed way, restricting themselves to first-hand, immediate experiences of the event. *United 93* depicts the highjacking of Flight 93 and the fear and resolve of the passengers on board in a form that can best be described as adrenalized stasis, the camera moving rapidly from static character to static character to capture the initial terror, the surreptitious tactical planning among the passengers, and their cathartic storming of the cockpit to try to seize control of the plane. Cutting between the scenes inside the aircraft and the frantic but wholly ineffective actions of air traffic control and the military on the ground, the film produces a seemingly documentary record of a single occurrence, and suggests in the process the seismic shift in the national reality that results. *World Trade Center*, directed by Oliver Stone, renders the events of 9/11 in a very different style, focusing on the grim experience of two firefighters trapped for thirteen hours in the pile of the World Trade Center. The true story of the last two survivors to be rescued from the rubble is rendered in an intensely claustrophobic manner, the survivors' physical immobility emphasized by almost motionless long takes. The only movement in certain drawn-out sequences is the movement of the two characters' mouths as they try to keep themselves conscious by talking. With occasional parallel sequences depicting the families and the friends of the two firefighters, the film contrasts these scenes of the anxious families, filled with both tension and color, with extended scenes under the pile, which become almost abstract studies in charcoal and ash. The agitational style typical of Oliver Stone gives way to a somber effort that might be compared to the "working through" of traumatic memory.

The Metahistorical Film

Certain films can be called metahistorical because they offer embedded or explicit critiques of the way history is conventionally represented. Although this approach to representing the historical past is rare in Hollywood, in many ways it highlights the cinema's potential for a critical, historiographic questioning of the past and its strengths as a form of thought experiment.

JFK (1991), directed by Oliver Stone, aroused intensive controversy for its blending of fictional and documentary techniques, and its radical practice of speculation and hypothesis in presenting a critique of the Warren Commission Report on John F. Kennedy's death. It presents a provocative interpretation of the assassination in a highly charged, polemical style that mixes idioms, splices together documentary and historical footage, and uses montage editing to disorient and "agitate" the viewer in a manner that calls into question accepted interpretations of the past.

Clint Eastwood's Flags of Our Fathers (2006) exposes the public relations campaign that followed the famous photo of the flag-raising over Iwo Jima, and the efforts to promote this image as a national icon. It provides a sobering account of the gulf between the actual event – and the men involved – and the way the event was promoted by the government for the purpose of raising war bonds. Edward Zwick's Courage Under Fire (1996) uses multiple subjective flashbacks, each narration contradicting the others, to attempt to determine the circumstances that led to a female helicopter commander's death in the first Gulf War. The military establishment is seeking to award her a posthumous Medal of Honor, the first to be awarded to a female officer, but the eyewitness accounts of the soldiers under her command vary widely. The legitimizing narrative that would convey the leadership qualities of women in the military is concealed among a complicated array of inconsistent interpretations. Alex Cox's *Walker* (1987), which has been characterized as a postmodern historical film, brings present-day objects from consumer culture – computers, Coke cans, 1950s automobiles – into its collagelike narrative of the nineteenth-century adventurer, William Walker, who invaded Nicaragua with a band of mercenaries and had himself elected emperor.

These intricate and interesting movies depart from conventional approaches to history in the Hollywood film, but can be understood as part of another cinematic tradition, mainly European, of interrogating the process of historical representation, both in written and cinematic form. Hans-Jürgen Syberberg's *Hitler, A Film From Germany* (1978, also known as *Our Hitler*), for example, attempts to confront the German amnesia concerning Hitler and complicity in his crimes by rendering the phenomenon of Hitler's rise as a disorienting operatic production, calling to mind the German fascination and investment in opera. The film's extreme length (seven hours and nine minutes), its use of dolls, dummies, and caricatures – Hitler is portrayed variously as a house painter, as Chaplin's Great Dictator, as a Frankenstein monster, and as Parsifal – underscores the way historical events and characters take on meaning through the way they are presented in the media. The film illustrates the way historical facts, such as the genocide practiced by the Third Reich, can be made to seem operatic, trivial, commonplace, or distorted, and emphasizes the way the memory of Hitler continues to influence the German national psyche.

In a very different way, Rossellini's series of nondramatic "history lessons" can also be seen as metahistorical works. In a series of films made late in his career, Rossellini explored the lives and times of various historical personages in a studiously nondramatic, non-psychologized way. His films *The Rise to Power of Louis XIV* (1966), *Socrates* (1970), and *The Age of the Medici* (1972) are made with nonprofessional actors and avoid following the dramatic arc of most fictional historical films. He attempts to capture the daily round of life in past historical times, bringing an almost documentary approach to the treatment of the past. Here Rossellini highlights the fact that we are viewing the past from a particular point of view with emphatic zoom shots drawing our attention to the presence of the camera in the reenactment of the historical past.

The Costume Film

The costume drama can be distinguished from other variants of the historical film by virtue of its fictional basis – its plot is most often based on a fictional literary source, and it does not depend on actual historical events as its main focus or framing material. Nevertheless, the costume drama provides many pleasures for viewers, for it often features a sumptuous re-creation of a historical period and setting, with the density of detail in the costumes and décor providing a source of sensual pleasure that equates history with emotion and passion.[25] In the 1940s the Gainsborough Studio produced a number of notable costume dramas, including adaptations of literary works such as *The Man in Grey* (1943), *Fanny by Gaslight* (1944), and *The Wicked Lady* (1945). Recent examples of the costume drama, such as *The Mark of Zorro* (1998), *Dangerous Liaisons* (1988), and *Marie Antoinette* (2006), employ historical settings for their aesthetic value, allowing the viewer to become a voyeur of the past. Historical films in general appeal to this emotional, voyeuristic interest on the part of the spectator, but the costume film allows its fullest expression, untrammeled by the sociopolitical conflicts that dominate the plots of films that deal with actual historical events.

The historical film emerged as a strong genre form very early in cinema history, and has renewed itself many times over the course of the twentieth and twenty-first centuries. Although the world of the past is its subject, the genre is often in the vanguard in terms of visual style and cinematic technique. The dramatic, compelling portraits of the past that are brought to life in the historical film have made it one of the most prestigious as well as one of the most controversial genres in film. It provides both a lens onto the past, which it frequently re-creates with exquisite attention to detail and period style, while also reflecting the cultural sensibility of the period in which it was made. Above all, the historical film provides an emotional connection to history in a way that foregrounds the power and importance of the past in shaping the cultural imaginary in the present.

Notes

1 As Robert Sklar writes, "If the cinema was something new for spectators of the 1890s, seeing larger-than-life projections of still and moving images was not." Exhibitions included magic lantern shows, dioramas, panoramas, and various forms of mechanically produced illusion. Some of the most successful and impressive of these projections were the Phantasmagoria and the Théâtre Optique. See Robert Sklar, *Film: An International History of the Medium* (New York: Harry N. Abrams, 2002): 16–24.
2 See Alison Griffiths, " 'Shivers Down Your Spine': Panoramas and the Origins of the Cinematic Reenactment," *Screen* 44(1) (2003): 1–37.

3   John Banvard, *Descriptions of Banvard's Geographical Painting of the Mississippi River* (New York: L. H. Bigelow, 1862). Quoted and cited in Griffiths, " 'Shivers Down Your Spine' ": 11.

4   Griffiths, p. Griffiths, " 'Shivers Down Your Spine' ": 20.

5   " 'Ben-Hur' Passes Over to the Movies," January 7, 1923.

6   See James Castonguay, "The Spanish-American War in United States Media Culture," http://chnm.gmu.edu/aq/.

7   Ibid.

8   Sklar, *Film*: 56.

9   Robert Rosenstone, *History on Film/Film on History* (Harlow, England and New York: Pearson Education, 2006): 13.

10 Richard Schickel, *D. W. Griffith: An American Life* (New York: Simon & Schuster, 1984): 270.

11 Robert Eberwein, ed. *The War Film* (New Brunswick, NJ: Rutgers University Press, 2005): 2–3.

12 Laurence Suid, *Guts & Glory: Great American War Movies* (Reading, MA: Addison-Wesley, 1978): 142.

13 Derek Elley, *The Epic Film: Myth and History* (London: Routledge & Kegan Paul, 1984): 6.

14 Ibid., 12, 13.

15 Quoted in Rosenstone, *History on Film*: 91.

16 Leo Lowenthal, "Biographies in Popular Magazines," in *1942–43*, ed. Paul Lazarsfeld and Frank Stanton (New York: Duel, Sloan & Pearce, 1944). Quoted in George Custen, *Bio/Pics: How Hollywood Constructed Public History* (New Brunswick, NJ: Rutgers University Press, 1992): 32.

17 Custen, *Bio/Pics*: 32–4.

18 See Mark E. Neely, Jr., "The Young Lincoln: Two Films," in Mark C. Carnes, ed., Past Imperfect: History According to the Movies (New York: Henry Holt, 1995): 124–7.

19 David Bordwell, *The Cinema of Eisenstein* (New York: Routledge, 2005): 224.

20 John Sayles, "A Conversation with Eric Foner and John Sayles," in Carnes, *Past Imperfect*: 13.

21 For a careful analysis of Collingwood's philosophy of history, see Paul Ricoeur, "The Reality of the Historical Past," (Milwaukee, WI: Marquette University Press, 1984).

22 Martin Scorsese, "Manhattan Asylum," interview with Ian Christie, *Sight and Sound*, January 2003.

23 Quoted in Daniel Stashower, The Beautiful Cigar Girl: Mary Rogers, Edgar Allan Poe, and the Invention of Murder (New York: Dutton, 2006): 14.

24 See Natalie Zemon Davis, *Slaves on Screen: Film and Historical Vision* (Cambridge, MA: Harvard University Press: 2000): 136.

25 See Sue Harper, *Picturing the Past: The Rise and Fall of the British Costume Film* (London: British Film Institute, 1994).

CHAPTER 2

THE WAR FILM: *SAVING PRIVATE RYAN*

With the extraordinary authenticity of its battlefield sequences and its powerful evocation of nostalgia for the certainties of the "last good war," *Saving Private Ryan* resurrected the traditional war film, which had fallen into disrepute in the post-Vietnam period, and reestablished it as a major form in American cinema. Expressing in an indelible way the themes of sacrifice, duty, and courage that have come to define the cultural legacy of World War II, the film reinvigorated the genre codes and conventions of the war films of the past, and crystallized the widespread movement at the end of the twentieth century to remember and acknowledge the contributions of what has come to be known as "the greatest generation." It also, however, broke new ground in its filtering of the events of World War II through the lens of Holocaust remembrance, a perspective that adds a contemporary meaning to the events the film depicts. And it departs from the heroic conventions of the war film by painfully dramatizing the psychology of cowardice in battle, with no redemptive heroic action at the end. In this sense, the film both recalls the past and responds to the present in a new way, illustrating the way the "genre memory" of the war film provides a layered record of past uses while also drawing on more recent perspectives to reorient our understanding of the past.[1]

Much of the publicity surrounding the film has focused on its extraordinary battle sequences, which stand as the most violent, graphic, and impressive re-creations of modern warfare ever put to film. André Bazin writes that "war, with its harvest of corpses, its immense destruction, its innumerable migrations, its concentration camps, its atomic bombs, leaves far behind it the art of imagination which had purported to reconstruct it."[2] In the case of *Saving Private Ryan*, however, the art of imagination seems to have closed the gap with the reality of war. In the D-Day, Omaha Beach sequence that inaugurates the work's main story, the film blends computer-generated imagery, live action photography, reenactments of documentary photographs and sequences, accelerated editing, slow-motion cinematography, and electronically enhanced sound design in an adrenalized montage that has been described as "pure cinema, at its most hypnotic and intense."[3] Through the use of destabilizing visual and acoustic techniques, *Saving Private Ryan* establishes a powerful claim to battlefield authenticity and realism, a claim that has been buttressed by the supporting testimony of veterans of D-Day concerning the accuracy of the film's depiction of combat.[4]

Saving Private Ryan's innovative use of technology places it in a long tradition of war films that have broken new ground in terms of special effects, creative camera work, and mass choreography in the service of realism and emotional power. *The Longest Day, All Quiet on the Western Front, The Birth of a Nation*, and the aviation warfare film *Hell's Angels* all established new camera and optical techniques, and set new standards for realism in film. Where *Saving Private Ryan* departs from the traditional war film, however, is in the brutality and graphic nature of its depiction of both mechanized and interpersonal violence. Where older combat films, especially those from the World War II era, presented an extremely sanitized and bloodless depiction of battle, *Saving Private Ryan* provides an extraordinary catalog of gruesome and fatal wounds and insists on bearing witness to the pain and trauma of dying. The maimed bodies, disfigured faces, detached limbs, and the sights and sounds of bullets and knives penetrating the flesh are presented as the inescapable reality of combat. The focus on the agony and fear of the soldiers gives rise to a different set of messages than those traditionally associated with the war film. Rather than serving as a conventional vehicle for patriotic ideals, the film communicates a sense of the terror and human cost of war, a stance that resulted in its being criticized for its refusal to articulate a higher justification for the fighting of World War II. Its terrifying battle depictions and its devastating images of the wounded and dead also led to protests over ABC's plans to screen the film on network television during the Iraq occupation and insurgency, protests that ABC heeded by pulling it off the schedule. *Saving Private Ryan*, in marked contrast to the conventions of the traditional war film, asks the audience to bear witness to the physical experience and horror of war before providing a rationale and justification for it. And the case it builds for the legitimacy of war is one that takes an unusual course, moving through evocations of Lincoln, the Holocaust, and the Bible. After a generation of antiwar films in response to Vietnam, *Saving Private Ryan* makes its case for the legitimacy of war in a way that brings both old and new perspectives on the American historical imaginary into view.

The war film consistently works into its narrative fabric a certain paradox: the release of violence and aggression, the suspension of civilized norms, the cultivation and training of the soldier's body as a "killing machine," are continually juxtaposed against the values of civilization, the norms of restraint and self-control. The sole authority of the state to wage war, to authorize aggression, is emphasized in the war film through military codes and the authority of the command hierarchy. Excessive violence, bloodlust, revenge, outright sadism are depicted as repugnant and ordinarily associated only with the enemy. At several points, however, *Saving Private Ryan* depicts American soldiers breaking a kind of internalized compact with civilization, transgressing an internalized code of behavior. At other times the film depicts soldiers who cannot enact the violence and aggression that is demanded of them. The film continually poses the question of the cost of violence, the cost to the soldier's sense of self-worth, but also dramatizes the costs of nonviolence as well. Twice, the main character, Captain Frank Miller, looks directly into the camera, implicating the viewer, insisting that we as audience weigh our own emotions and assess our own convictions.[5]

This is foregrounded in the film in the opening scenes, as the film frames the story of Captain Miller through a visit to the Normandy cemetery where American soldiers who perished in the D-Day invasion are buried. As the camera follows an older man walking with his family into the cemetery, the camera details in a long tracking shot the seemingly endless rows of crosses, and one Jewish star, that mark the graves of the soldiers. The man seems to find the grave he is looking for, and drops to his knees. Standing behind him, the female members of his family are given special prominence. As the camera begins moving closer, the older character begins crying, the camera moves into an extreme close-up of his eyes, and the scene cuts to windy, rainy, bleak-looking seacoast. A graphic title informs us that this is June 6, 1943, and the place is Omaha Beach, Green Dog Sector.

As the D-Day landing begins, the film provides a series of visceral portraits of fear and sick apprehension. The soldiers on the landing craft are shown vomiting, crossing themselves, praying, and communing with their consciences. The film's lead character, Captain Miller, is no exception: his right hand is shaking uncontrollably; his face reveals a sense of embarrassment in a quick eyeline exchange with his sergeant. All of these shots are in close-up, with no exterior shots to orient the viewer. The moment the landing craft ramp door falls open, the soldiers are shredded by bullets that seem preternaturally well aimed: one soldier after the other falls with a wound to the head, to the chest, the front ranks falling and exposing the next row of soldiers. None of the sounds of gunfire are audible; we hear only the impact of the bullets as they lodge themselves in the soldiers' flesh or ricochet into the landing craft: they seem to originate from the atmosphere itself. Some soldiers jump over the side of the craft to escape the bullets. They are shown underwater struggling with their equipment, the weight of it dragging them to the bottom, drowning them in the ocean. Bullets course through the water, seeming almost harmless in their slowed momentum, hypnotic, until they strike two soldiers underwater and immediately the screen is flooded with blood.

FIGURE 2.1 The first battle in *Saving Private Ryan*, the assault on the beach (1998) [Paramount Pictures/Photofest]

In its initial moments, the scene alternates among almost silent shots underwater and shots from the soldier's perspective above the water, and is dominated by the sound of bullets thumping into flesh, whizzing by, or ricocheting against the steel of the boat. A third series of shots convey the point of view of a German machine-gunner, with complete optical control of the space. The opposition between visual mastery from above and the disorientation and helplessness below creates a striking sense of impossible odds, as if the invasion could not possibly succeed. The rapid panning, jarring cutting, and extreme alternation of angles are joined to a soundtrack that engulfs the sonic space in confusion. The rapid-fire images and sounds create what looks like a kind of paralysis on the part of the soldiers, who inch forward as if numbed by the assault. Pulling a soldier along with him, Miller drags himself to the shore. The soldier with Miller takes a bullet to the heart as Miller looks at him, and slides away into the ocean. At this point, Miller himself slides into a kind of trance. The camera begins to render his subjective viewpoint, depicting the action in jerky stop-motion, conveying the sounds of the battle in a muffled, unfocused way, depicting Miller as if in a dream-state. Filtered through Miller's mindscreen, the film depicts the initial moments of the landing as a Goyaesque catalog of disasters: men consumed by flames, limbs flying from bodies, men searching for and carrying away their severed body parts. The stop-motion cinematography and muffled soundtrack render these scenes as otherworldly, distorted, defamiliarized: as we register the events, we have a paradoxical sense that the experience is impossible to represent; traumatic; it seems as if the film is asking us simply to bear witness with Miller, a point that is powerfully reinforced when Miller looks directly into the camera in close-up.

Several critics have discussed the theme of witnessing in connection with the depiction of traumatic historical events. As A. Susan Owen writes, "Spielberg's call to commemorate in *Saving Private Ryan* is constructed through the visual act or metaphor of witnessing. Various acts of witnessing constitute the key moments in the film."[6] Miller, at both the beginning and the end of the film, is dramatically foregrounded as witness to near-traumatizing events, as the camera renders his consciousness as if he were stunned. Drawn into his subjective viewpoint, we can see, in a staggered, stop-motion sort of way, but we cannot hear. Both at the beginning and at the end of the film, the audience is positioned as if receiving another's act of witnessing.

E. Ann Kaplan has written extensively on the representation of trauma in the cinema, and in particular, on the motif or device of witnessing as a variation on point-of-view editing, a move away from the feminist preoccupation with the gaze and its associations with voyeurism and scopophilia.[7] The structural importance of this device in *Saving Private Ryan* flows from Miller's direct visual address to the audience, a device that inscribes the audience into a relay system of looks that asserts its status as truth. The look of Miller into the camera has the effect of predicating the events depicted, asserting their value as authentic, making the film's representation of war a kind of testimony. Although war films have often used unusual and highly expressive techniques to underline the truth value of their portrayal of conflict – ranging from voiceover narration, the use of inserted maps, the inclusion of documentary sequences, location shooting, and occasionally the use of extras who had actually participated in the events – the film's foregrounding of the act of witnessing produces a sense of heightened significance. The film deviates from the norms of cinematic narrative discourse with its direct address to the camera in order to suggest a form of testimony, bound by the rules of veridical rather than fictional discourse.

After Miller looks into the camera, it cuts to a direct point-of-view shot of a young soldier. The sound gradually comes back into focus, as we hear him shouting "What the hell should we do now, Sir?" As the men under Miller's command slowly advance up the beach, trying to get to the seawall that will offer some protection, the camera continues to record hellish images of impossibly grisly wounds. One soldier is calling for his mother, another wounded man dragged by Miller toward safety has the lower part of his body severed by a shell. Several incidents stand out. In one, a medic, directly exposed to fire, finally stops the internal bleeding of a soldier shot in the gut. At the moment that he shouts that he has stopped the bleeding – a small success in the midst of unrelenting bloodshed – a bullet penetrates the helmet of the wounded man. Another especially vivid scene revolves around the radio: Miller tells the radio operator to let headquarters know that the beach is not secure, that "Dog One" cannot be used for the landing of tanks. As Miller turns back to the radio operator to give him further instructions, he sees that his face has entirely disappeared. The man's head remains, but the face is now a smoking, concave depression. Another instance is the "lucky bastard" whose helmet has just saved him from a bullet. As he takes the helmet off to examine the bullet hole, another shot penetrates his head.

A great deal of critical attention has been given to the powerful verisimilitude of the combat scenes in Saving Private Ryan. Audiences were asked to prepare themselves for the graphic quality of the film's opening sequence. The history of the Hollywood war film, however, is replete with similar claims of verisimilitude, claims which dominated the publicity for *The Birth of a Nation*, *All Quiet on the Western Front*, and *The Longest Day*, among many others. The hyperrealistic representation of combat is an important, perhaps essential characteristic of the war film. While historical films in general tend to strive for a sense of authenticity, the reenactment of combat scenes in the war film seems to be a special case of mimetic discourse.

The re-presentation of combat scenes in a public setting was also a major form of entertainment in the century preceding cinema. Dioramas and panoramas, enormously popular in the nineteenth century, were often dedicated to reconstructions of famous battles. The rendering of these battle scenes in gigantic, 360-degree paintings, replete with lighting effects, music, and narration, can clearly be seen as a precursor to widescreen cinema. And their mode of address to spectators is comparable also. As Alison Griffiths writes:

> Audiences attending the typical nineteenth-century battle panorama would not only have been entertained by the spectacular painting but would have been interpellated into the roles of historical witness or war reporter. The ability to re-experience an event of enormous national significance, to step inside history . . . were doubtless intended to trigger feelings of nationalistic fervor [created by] the transformation of war into visual spectacle.[8]

The literature of the time described the effects these enormous panoramas had on spectators: Griffiths continues:

> for some spectators, the illusion may have become "unbearable," forcing them to leave the painting sooner than they had intended. There are numerous accounts of nineteenth century spectators becoming faint or dizzy when looking at a panorama . . . newspaper accounts went so far as to advise ladies of a nervous disposition to be on their guard when viewing panoramas lest the experience become overwhelming.[9]

And the images painted on the panorama were often highly sensational. The description of a an image of a ship exploding, the highlight of the panorama depicting the Battle of the Nile, for example, is reminiscent of the Omaha Beach sequence in *Saving Private Ryan*: "Perhaps no words can fully convey an impression of this inferno . . . Clinging to the masts and yardarms in desperate contortions are the poor sailors; some have been torn to pieces and catapulted into the air by the explosion; heads, limbs, cannon mounts, yards, masts, muskets, crates, shreds of ropes and all the other contents of the ship rain down on all sides."[10]

The mimetic visualization of combat in nineteenth-century panoramas clearly prepared spectators for the cinematic genre of the war film, and created expectations of verisimilitude and spectacle in the filmic treatments of battle scenes. One of the key aspects of this re-presentation in both film and the panorama, however, is that the reenactment not only recalls the original event, but also "reforms" it, enhancing its visuality, improving the view of the event, offering a multi-perspectival rendering that offers detailed description, broad overviews, and a multitude of sharply etched moments. Moreover, the striking impression of verisimilitude in combat films serves a particular type of rhetorical argument; the weight of the experience, the amplified impression of reality, implies that the event is worth revisiting, that it has national significance.

Double-Voicing

One of the most sharply etched moments of the opening combat scene in *Saving Private Ryan* also serves to express a sense of national purpose, a sense of historical ideology. This theme emerges principally through the character of the sharpshooter, Jackson. The sharpshooter is distinguished from the other characters in the film. He is from the South, he does not look disheveled or combat-weary, he quotes scripture and calls on the Lord before he takes aim, and he sleeps peacefully at night. Moreover, he dies heroically in a church tower. In the opening scenes, he is called upon to take out the German machine-gun nest, an especially difficult assignment. As the gunfire and explosions that had rocked the screen throughout the opening sequence subside, Jackson kisses his crucifix, begins a prayer, takes aim, and delivers a fatal shot. The camera provides an extreme close-up on the pulling of the trigger, and then cuts to a shot of the falling German gunner. Cutting immediately away from the sharpshooter to the main battle on the beach, we see an army chaplain giving the last rites, and then another soldier huddled on the beach, wounded, and reciting the rosary. We then return to Jackson, who offers another prayer and takes out the remaining two German gunners with a single shot.

The act of killing is thus bracketed by prayer: the chaplain, the rosary, and shots of Jackson kissing his crucifix serve to reframe the killing, to resacralize the gun, and to reunite the gun with a sense of high moral purpose. After a decade of Vietnam films in which combat and killing were largely associated with atrocity, with dehumanizing and vicious acts, the gun in *Saving Private Ryan* is rehabilitated as a symbolic object through Jackson. The resacralizing of the gun aligns sacred and national purpose, as the audience looks, as if through Jackson's sight, to watch the German soldiers fall. *Saving Private Ryan*, Owens argues persuasively, restores an American vision of righteous destruction, what Richard Slotkin has called "regeneration through violence."[11] Combat here becomes, once again, an honorable contest of skill and chance. As Owens suggests, it transforms the act of killing into an art form. The film recenters American moral authority in modern warfare, restoring legitimacy to mythic images of American power and creating a shared vision of national destiny.

Saving Private Ryan displays in a striking way the characteristic that Bakhtin calls "double voicing" – the adapting of an older genre to a new context.[12] It works both to rehabilitate the war film after Vietnam, as well as providing a new, contemporary perspective on the past. Many critics of the film did not take this double voice into account, arguing that the film did not do justice to the high moral purpose that motivated American soldiers and the American cause in World War II. The lack of patriotic speeches, the absence of explicit moral justification, the fact that there are no references to freedom from oppression, removes, for these critics, any potential patriotic message from the film. As Peter Ehrenhaus says, it seems to "privatize patriotism by divorcing it from its proper, political context."[13] Instead, the film hurls us immediately into graphic scenes of carnage, and depicts American soldiers joking while they kill German soldiers who are in the act of surrendering. Near-mutinies, scenes of soldiers overcome by fear and cowardice, the absence of any overarching message, undermine the conventional narrative of civilization as an interpretive context. Other critics, however, fault the film for romanticizing war. For these critics, the film indulges in uncritical fawning over the "Greatest Generation," reinforcing the nostalgia industry that had developed around this period in the United States. The powerful kinaesthetic spectacle of its combat scenes, moreover, were seen as all too exciting and emotionally gripping, dynamic and thrilling examples of pure cinema, a portrait of combat that rehabilitates the good name of war for a later generation.

Both strands of criticism – the lack of patriotism argument and the glorifying of war argument – reveal the shaping influence of the Vietnam period and the Vietnam film on depictions of war. After Vietnam, war was seen as corrupt, without redemptive value, as an experience of collective loss. In this context, the image of an integrative national community bound by a social compact, by common interests and obligations,

FIGURE 2.2 Captain Miller (Tom Hanks) as the citizen-soldier in *Saving Private Ryan* (1998) [Paramount Pictures/Photofest]

no longer seems viable. For most critics, the film seems to fall short both on the patriotic side and on the critical side, providing neither a satisfying patriotic revivification of war nor being sufficiently critical of the excesses and brutality of war in general.

By keeping the idea of double voicing in mind, however, we see how the film serves a complex ideological function, serving both to "reillusion" American national identity while at the same time paying homage to the accomplishments of "the Greatest Generation."[14] Erenhaus argues that Spielberg constructs a moral justification for the war by redefining it as a moral crusade against the horrors of the Holocaust. Although he considers this an implausible historical argument – this was not the reason the United States went to war – it functions in contemporary US culture in terms of a broader symbolic argument. The Holocaust has become a marker of the premier moral failing of Western, Christian culture, a "benchmark for personal and collective moral judgments and responsibilities."[15] The film, in Ehrenhaus's reading, reimagines the war as a national quest against the Holocaust, foregrounding the Jewish soldier Mellish, and making Mellish's death struggle against a Nazi SS officer a key moral and symbolic event in the film.

Holocaust memory is woven into the narrative. An early underscoring of this theme occurs just after the storming of the beach sequence, as the soldiers under Miller's command sort through the weapons and effects of the dead German soldiers. One soldier finds a Hitler Youth knife on a young German soldier, and hands it to Mellish. Mellish responds with a quip, "And now it's a Shabbat Challah knife," before breaking down in tears. As Mellish tries to stifle and conceal his emotion, the camera dwells on the faces of the other soldiers, in particular Sergeant Horvath, who regards him with sympathy. Horvath then scoops up some dirt from the ground, seals it into a canister marked "Normandy" and places it in his pack, along with canisters labeled "Africa" and "Italy."

The scene brings several messages into the foreground. First, it identifies the German soldier as very young. Although the Germans have viciously pounded the American troops in the opening scene, the face of the dead German soldier, who looks to be about 16 years old, is the first German whose features are actually visible. But overriding this detail is the association the Hitler Youth knife establishes with the Holocaust. Mellish's comment makes this explicit; his emotional breakdown is inexplicable unless we assume he is responding to knowledge of the Nazi death camps, and that this knowledge is shared among the troops. The scene cues us to the extent that Holocaust memory will be woven into the film. In Ehrenhaus's reading, the memory of the Holocaust plays a role in the major plot line of the film, the "saving" of Private Ryan, as it reminds us of the theme of *Schindler's List*, "Whoever saves one life, saves the entire world."

Mellish's response gives us an extended scene in which male emotion is prominent. Although the prelude to the landing emphasizes the fear and apprehension of the soldiers, here another theme comes to the fore. Throughout, the film invests in two agendas: male emotion, desire, friendship, and vulnerability versus duty, honor, and heroism. The friction between these two agendas creates a striking form of male melodrama, as scenes of male emotion, vulnerability, and tears far outnumber scenes that overtly express traditionally male war themes of honor and patriotism. The tearful incidents in the film outweigh portrayals of the stoic pursuit of male duty. The two agendas are brought together in the theme of sacrifice: a willingness to sacrifice the self for the group brings vulnerability and heroism together, fusing the two.[16]

Both these themes, emotion and duty, are tied to the figure of the woman. Images of mothers, references to wives, the song recording by Edith Piaf, place much of the film under the sign of the maternal and the feminine. Scenes of intense emotional distress repeatedly cycle back to evocations of mothers. The repeated references to "earning this," earning the right to return home, is associated with the feminine; the killing, destruction, and aggression that the war demands is justified not, as is typical, by patriarchal law or order, but rather by the appeal to the feminine. Sacrifice is associated with earning the right to return, to the feminine, and to the mother.

"A Piece of the American Bible"

The film marks the transition to this theme, and to the second major movement of the film, with a close-up shot of Captain Miller surveying Omaha Beach from above, his face registering an ambiguous set of emotions. Sergeant Horvath, from off-screen, says "It's quite a view, isn't it, Sir?" Miller responds that yes, it is quite a view, a comment that seems to herald a view of some form of sublime landscape. Instead, the camera begins detailing in medium close-up the watery graveyard the beach has become, with soldiers strewn amid floating boxes of equipment, a multitude of dead fish, and red water. The camera edges along the beach, and tracks in on the body of one soldier, whose backpack reveals the name S. Ryan.

In this series of shots, the film cues us to remember the opening sequence in the Normandy cemetery, and to recall the face of the man whose memory authorizes these images of the past. The close-up of Captain Miller here and the close-up of the older man at the beginning of the film are framed in a similar way; moreover, the camera's surveying of the dead on the beach recalls the tracking shots of crosses in the cemetery. The physical proximity of the cemetery to the battlefield provides a further sense of the connection between these two scenes. The shot of the dead soldier named Ryan then fades to a scene set in an office, where the names of the dead are being assembled. Here, we track among long rows of female typists, as the letters written to the parents of the dead are heard in a voiceover montage of different officers' voices, underlining the individual nature of the condolence letters, and the sincerity of their contents. Three brothers have been killed on the same day. A fourth brother, the eponymous Private Ryan, will become the object of the search that forms the remainder of the film's story.

First reading, then quoting from memory a letter from Abraham Lincoln to a grieving mother who had lost five sons on the battlefield during the Civil War, the famous "Bixby letter," the film depicts General George C. Marshall ordering a search for Private Ryan, who has parachuted into Normandy with his unit, the 101st Airborne. Carl Sandberg has called this letter "a piece of the American Bible."[17] In this scene, the film explicitly invokes a patriotic, elevated form of representation, a ceremonial style missing from the rest of the film. The scenes with General Marshall, the voiceover readings of the letters of regret from commanding officers, and the short, mute scene of Mrs. Ryan about to receive the news about her three sons, evoke a national context that is idealized, explicitly commemorative, drawn from the visual lexicon of an Andrew Wyeth or even a Norman Rockwell. Nevertheless, the reading and quotation from Lincoln resonate in the larger symbolic structure of the text. Lincoln has often been represented as a kind of maternal figure in American culture, a leader who healed the nation's wounds, preserved the Union, and folded the former Confederate States into his embrace. Here, the appeal to Lincoln as a kind of higher authority, defining the purpose served by the deaths of the soldiers as a "sacrifice on the altar of freedom," merges the sacred and the secular. As Sacvan Berkovitch writes, "Only in the United States has nationalism carried with it the Christian meaning of the sacred . . . Only America has united nationality and universality, civic and spiritual selfhood, secular and redemptive history, the country's past and the paradise to be in a single synthetic ideal."[18] In *Saving Private Ryan*, the Christian-national ideal is complemented by the Judaic principle, "no action is more powerful than affirming the value of a single human life."[19] The film strives to construct a new secular covenant, ecumenical, in Ehrenhaus's formulation, fusing Jewish and Christian principles in a re-enabling of American national identity.

The middle portion of the film concentrates on the foot-patrol search for Private Ryan in the fields and villages of Normandy. Here, stereotypes familiar from past war films are plainly evident in the ethnic composition of the patrol: the smart-mouthed New Yorker, the rural southerner, the solid Midwesterner, the fully assimilated Jewish soldier. The range of personalities is also familiar, ranging from the cynical, to the idealistic, to the respectful. But as the foot patrol moves deeper into the country, the film again seems to exhibit the double voice of an older genre adapted for the present. The soldiers are openly mocking of Corporal Upham, a journalist recruited into the patrol to serve as a translator. His literary, poetic conception of war, especially his quotations from Emerson about the bond that emerges among soldiers in combat, brings him scorn. The soldiers in the patrol question their orders and their mission, unwilling to accept the rationale that the eight of them should jeopardize their lives to preserve the life of one enlisted man. And the cost of the mission is made plain early on when one of them is killed by a sniper while he is attempting a humanitarian deed, trying, against Miller's orders, to help a little French girl whose parent are desperate for her to travel in the ostensible safety of the platoon.

The sentimental, ceremonial discourse of family, Lincoln, motherhood, and sacrifice from the scenes in Washington a few moments before is almost immediately repudiated by the soldiers themselves, who are repelled by Upham's poetic notion of combat and who openly question the mission itself. The core question that structures the middle portion of the narrative is the question of authority – will the code of military discipline hold? And what are the motivations for maintaining this code? Steven Spielberg has said that after Vietnam, war films have become intensely personal; people fight just to survive, or to save the guy next to them. He also has said that no American filmmaker can any longer tell a morally unambiguous story of warfare, and that *Saving Private Ryan* is a morality play. And it is the story of the enlisted man that needs to be told. In order to narrate this story, the citizen–soldier must be reimagined as an honorable and brave public servant, and distinguished from the cynicism and the psychopathology of the Vietnam vet.

Steve Neale has described two distinct narrative trajectories in the American war film revolving around authority, omniscience, and narrative motivation.[20] Some films, such as *Paths of Glory* and *Objective Burma*, depict an open conflict of interest between those giving the orders and the troops enacting them. In *Paths of Glory*, the generals are portrayed as irrational and contemptuous of the troops, sending them into battle for personal or ill-conceived reasons. The spectator is aware of the generals' motives, although the troops are not. In *Objective Burma*, the command hierarchy is depicted as callous and uncaring, but not malevolent. The troops are "in the dark" as to the planning or rationale for their movements and assignments, and begin to lose confidence, but the orders they are given eventually lead to a successful conclusion. Other films, such as *Platoon*, *Steel Helmet*, and *A Walk in the Sun*, are limited in their point-of-view structure to the soldiers on patrol. The spectator is not given access to the thinking or planning behind the mission; just like the characters, the audience is very limited in knowledge. As the mission encounters difficulties and experiences losses, there is an erosion of confidence, but there is no explicit conflict of agendas between the men on the ground and the leaders at the top.

Saving Private Ryan is a hybrid of these two structures. Although we witness General Marshall giving the order to rescue Ryan, and are reassured as to the benevolent rationale behind the mission, the main thrust of the film, including the opening landing, is limited to the perspective of the combat soldiers. The conflict of interest that Neale describes as a feature of explicitly antiwar films such as *Paths of Glory* is, however, not present here. Rather, the mission itself comes to seem increasingly misguided, despite its humanitarian intent. The death of one soldier for attempting a similar humanitarian mission to the saving of Ryan spells this out. The obstacles the soldiers encounter, the loss of members of their troop, heated disagreements about their course of action, and the sheer difficulty of finding Ryan bring Miller's patrol close to the breaking point.

Saving Private Ryan diminishes the role of external, abstract motivations such as duty, honor, or patriotism as the motive for carrying out the mission. Instead, the drive to complete the mission comes from inside: each member of the troop seems to find his own reason for pushing forward. In the Vietnam film *Apocalypse Now*, Captain Willard moves into a psychological zone in which the orders he follows are no longer relevant to him; he tells us in voiceover that he is "no longer in their Army," that his mission no longer matters, that he is responding to another imperative, one that has slowly emerged in the long river journey into the jungle. Nevertheless, he performs his role as designated assassin, out of a sense of fatalism, perhaps, or psychosis. The military project and the command structure are here portrayed as deviant, perverse, and immoral. In *Saving Private Ryan*, however, the integrity of the military project and military command structure is threatened but reestablished in an original variation on the questions of duty, hierarchical order, and sacrifice, a variation that departs from both the conventional war film as well as the antiwar film.

As Sergeant Horvath and Private Reiban square off, a conflict that brings the soldiers to the brink of mutiny, Miller begins to tell the patrol his biographical history, a subject of much debate and a growing pool of bets among the company. He was a high-school English composition teacher. He coached the high-school baseball team, and everyone felt he was well suited to his job. Over here, however, his previous life is a mystery, perhaps even to himself. He wonders aloud if he will ever be that self again. But he holds the thought that perhaps he can earn his way back, that for all the killing he has done and for all the men he has lost, perhaps by finding Ryan he can earn his way back. But he knows for sure that with every man he kills, he is further away.

Miller's confession defines the mission in extremely personal terms. He doesn't care about Ryan, "who's just a name," but he does care about getting back to his wife, and whether she will even recognize him. This mission may help him find his way back to his former self. He then offers to release any of the soldiers who want to go back to the main company. Unlike the traditional war film, Miller here describes his motivation for fighting as a re-enobling of the self, a reaffirmation of self. Rather than the external motivation of a higher cause, in which duty and sacrifice are motivated by adherence to an external code, Miller defines duty and sacrifice in terms of personal reparation. And unlike the Vietnam film, such as *Born on the Fourth of July* or *Full Metal Jacket*, the loss of self is not blamed on the dehumanizing experiences of military life or the built-in opposition between the military command and the soldiers on the ground. Miller's revelation of self here belongs to another genre of discourse, one that Owens describes as a feminine confessional mode, a conversational mode of intimate self-disclosure, privileging reflective speech over action. Considered as a reimagining of the American citizen-soldier, the interactions the soldiers have with Miller are a postmodern mixture of gender nostalgia and post-feminism, an ideologically innovative configuration of masculinity within the conventions of the combat film. Miller reconciles generational differences in styles of masculinity; he is sensitive and vulnerable, but also resourceful and responsible. He is dedicated to duty, yet disdainful of romanticized idealizations of war. He combines both male and female attributes: conventional masculine leadership and a feminized conversational style.

He controls the possible mutiny unfolding here and ensures honorable behavior by linking actions to a higher ethos, to "home:" "Every man I kill, the farther from home I feel."

At the same time, however, the gun and the act of killing must be resacralized as a legitimate instrument of the state. The larger cultural project of the film, its re-enobling of American national identity after Vietnam, must be articulated through the blood rhetoric of war, despite the unusual foregrounding of personal disclosure. Although the powerful evocation of Miller as a citizen-soldier reminiscent of an earlier period of American history restores a sense of personal integrity to the particular mission defined as "saving" Private Ryan, the larger question of national purpose, the articulation of a national covenant that would justify the sacrifice of life and limb and resacralize the gun remains unarticulated.

The film is divided into three major movements: the opening landing sequence, the foot patrol in search of Ryan, and the defense of the bridge at Remelle. Reversing the trajectory of the Vietnam film, *Saving Private Ryan* begins with the motif of survival and gradually acquires the thematic values associated with World War II – dedication to principles of self-sacrifice in the service of a larger cause. The question that shadows the first two movements of the film, however, is precisely the nature of that larger cause. The opening landing sequence is dominated by a sense of visceral, meaningless violence, what Dana Polan calls "noncumulative explosions of violence that lead nowhere and mean nothing."[21] In the middle portion of the film, the post-Vietnam mood of cynicism and skepticism regarding any sense of national community defines much of the action. The camaraderie among the patrol is itself undermined by their distrust concerning the legitimacy of their mission. As Ehrenhaus writes, "Vietnam memory works against the image of an integrative national community bound by common interests and obligations."[22]

Reillusioning America

The complex ideological and cultural work of the film is fully realized in the film's climactic scene, in which a critical bridge is held by the American soldiers in the face of overwhelming German firepower. Here, *Saving Private Ryan* explicitly weaves Holocaust memory into its portrayal of World War II; it is the hallowed ground on which the mission is conducted. In Mellish's agonizing death struggle, the historical justification for World War II is concentrated in a single, hellish battle between a German and a Jew – perhaps the least bloody but most harrowing combat scene in the film. With the Holocaust constituting, for contemporary American culture, a central event of World War II – an emblematic expression of the evil of Nazi Germany – the film re-enobles the war and resacralizes the gun on the basis of a larger rescue operation. It is not just Private Ryan who will be rescued and restored to his grieving family, but an entire people. In the defeat of the Nazis, the American people will be redeemed.

Although the genocide of the Jews was a known fact in Washington during the war, the political and business establishment repeatedly failed to intervene in ways that could have been effective in limiting the slaughter of the Jews, a point that has become increasingly well established in American culture. In our contemporary understanding of the period, guilt and responsibility for the Holocaust lies not only or exclusively with the Nazis. *Saving Private Ryan* derives a complex symbolic resolution to the problem of recognizing American political complicity and cowardice in the face of this knowledge, while at the same time honoring the sacrifice and unity of American soldiers. In the many shades of meaning conveyed by the title of the film, *Saving Private Ryan* comes to represent a narrative of salvation on several levels.

Ehrenhaus calls the Holocaust the "grand moral landscape, the ground upon which these characters search for Private Ryan."[23] After finally finding Ryan, who decides that he will remain with his unit, refusing to allow Miller to bring him back to the base – "these are the only brothers I have left" – Miller decides to reinforce the troops protecting the bridge from the Germans. The bridge in the town of Remelle is a key transit point, the only way across the river for the American or the German tanks. The mission of the soldiers is to hold the bridge until the American artillery can arrive, and to prevent the Germans from seizing the bridge and using it for their own tanks as they try to beat back the American assault in Normandy. Miller is the highest-ranking officer present, and quickly takes charge, deploying the troops, fixing charges to the bridge in case they have to blow it up to prevent the Germans from using it, and devising an improvised explosive device, a "sticky bomb," that will knock the treads off the German tanks. The long vigil the soldiers keep as they await the German and the American artillery is dominated by the playing of an Edith Piaf record on a phonograph, with Upham, the untested war correspondent, translating the verses. Here, the film again evokes a nostalgic sense of the feminine, and by extension, of homecoming, before the battle begins.

As the German tanks begin their inexorable push toward the bridge, the soundtrack is dominated by the sound of metal squealing against

FIGURE 2.3 Private Ryan (Matt Damon) in the ruins of Remielle, having gotten his direction home. *Saving Private Ryan* (1998) [Paramount Pictures/Photofest]

metal, the sound of enormous steel machines grinding away. The ensuing battle sequence cuts rapidly among soldiers stationed at various ambush sites: Jackson in the church steeple, Miller and Ryan on the bridge, Private Reiban who affixes "sticky bombs" to the wheels of the tanks. At first, the battle seems to go well. Jackson, praying before every shot, dispatches several German infantrymen from his perch in the church steeple. The "sticky bombs" prove effective, bringing several armored vehicles to a stop. But once the tanks take aim at Jackson and demolish the steeple, the tide seems to turn.

The extended scene of hand-to-hand combat between Mellish and a German officer stands as the crystallized expression of the film's reinvention of the war film. Stationed in an upstairs apartment, Mellish has run out of ammunition, and shouts for Upham, whose job it is to resuppy the soldiers, to bring him more. Upham, festooned with ammunition belts, stands outside paralyzed by fear and indecision. A lone German soldier breaks in on Mellish, and they begin a life-and-death struggle. Mellish screams for help, but Upham is unable to move. Mellish seems to have the advantage, and takes out his bayonet, at which point the stronger German officer begins to prevail. With excruciating slowness, he lowers the knife to Mellish's chest, overpowering Mellish with his superior strength. Mellish again screams for help, and again Upham, on the stairs a few feet from Mellish, does nothing. As the knife enters the chest and breaks the breastbone of Mellish, the Nazi officer speaks to him soothingly, almost like a mother, "Let's put an end to this. This will be easier for you. Much easier. It will soon be over. Shh, Shh."

The German soldier leaves and passes Upham on the stairs, barely taking note of him. In this shot, the SS insignia is clearly visible on his uniform. The SS, standing for the Schutzstaffel elite corps, ran the extermination camps and coordinated the Final Solution. Although it seems unlikely that an SS officer would be engaged in a front-line combat operation, the insignia embeds a specific reference to the Holocaust in a small detail of *mise en scène*. Upham serves as a synecdoche for American inaction concerning the camps: the scene can be read as a reference to American guilt for not having acted, for not having acted sooner, for not doing enough. The failure to actively and vigorously oppose the Nazi persecution of the Jews is emblematized in Upham's failure to act, to come to the rescue of Mellish.

By evoking the Holocaust in such a direct and unmistakable way, the film places it at the center of its project of commemoration. Holocaust memory, which has become heavily Americanized over the past fifteen years or so, becomes a way of rebuilding American national identity after

Vietnam. As Erenhaus says, "our inheritance in the present becomes a reconstituted national identity, leapfrogging back over Vietnam to draw moral clarity and commitment from the enormity of the horror it sought to end."[24]

The battle of Remelle ends with another sequence of direct address to the camera by Captain Miller. As the largest German tank approaches the bridge, Miller and Ryan are alone on the bridge. Ryan has been reduced to hysteria, sobbing, drawn into a fetal position, incapable of acting. Like Upham, he has been reduced to paralysis. Unlike Upham, however, we do not see Ryan filled with self-loathing and internal conflict: he is traumatized to the point that he has lost all capacity for decision or for action. Miller observes him, and the camera once again gives us his stunned, subjective viewpoint. Here again, Miller looks directly into the camera. At the beginning and at the end of the film, the audience is positioned as if "receiving another's testimony."[25] The interior frame of Miller's witnessing is again connected to the external narrative frame of Ryan's recollection. Wounded and unable to blow up the bridge, with Ryan incapable of acting and the German tank bearing down on him, Miller, in a seemingly futile gesture, empties his pistol at the tank. One of the bullets penetrates the viewing slot of the tank, causing a massive internal explosion. As Miller dies, he gives his final command to Ryan: "James, earn it. Earn this."

The implausible ending of the film, with Miller somehow taking out a tank with only a pistol while delivering Ryan to safety, reinstates the traditional victorious endings of World War II films, especially in the invocation to memory that is implied by Miller's words. Five of the eight main characters have died; three remain to commemorate the war. The ending of the film forms a striking contrast to the endings of Vietnam films and to the endings of World War I films. Vietnam combat films drive home their antiwar messages in their closing scenes: one thinks of *Apocalypse Now*, with Kurtz's whispered "The horror. The horror," as he dies, or *Full Metal Jacket*, which closes with a Marine patrol singing the Mickey Mouse Club theme song after having executed a young female sniper. Rather than a commemorative project, Vietnam films are characterized by a fear of contagion, a sense of spreading evil: they seek to inoculate the present by exposing the dishonor that was the past. Owens looks at Vietnam films as acts of lamentation. The films "rebuke us with visceral visions of a war that ravaged an ancient land and deeply damaged America."[26] And the ending is also unlike the endings of World War I films, which typically ended with no survivors, no one to commemorate the battles, and no explicit invocation of heroism or continuity with the past: as Pierre Sorlin writes, "when the film comes to an end, no one has been spared. It is like a world's end: no story can be told, there is not the possibility even of a history." In World War I films, no one cares to tell what had happened. There is no memory. The message of a world's end, of utter devastation, is delivered without comment by the filmmakers: "the emptiness of the end overwhelms the spectator: makes them feel as if they have been caught up in some vast, impersonal, meaningless disaster."[27]

Saving Private Ryan, in contrast, insists on commemoration. Like earlier World War II films in which there is always someone who survives to remember and tell the story, the film closes with an explicit recall of the sacrifices that the soldiers have made. But a mixed message emerges in the way Ryan, now an elderly man, is depicted in the cemetery. As the face of the young Ryan listening to Miller on the bridge morphs into the face of the elderly Ryan at the cemetery, the commemorative project set out by the film includes a message of mortification, and the posing of a question. Ryan is depicted on his knees in the cemetery. In tears, he appeals to his wife to assure him that he has "been a good man," that he has "led a good life"; in other words, that he has "earned this." Although his wife assures him, sincerely, the closing scene suggests the lamentation ritual of Vietnam films; with this ending, *Saving Private Ryan* evokes films such as *Gardens of Stone* and *The Deer Hunter*, voicing a theme much more characteristic of the Vietnam film than of World War II combat films, a theme that Polan describes as "confusion, contradiction, and struggles over meaning."[28] The final legitimation that earlier war films found in moments of conversion, moments when the personal convictions of the individual soldiers finally mesh with the larger national purpose, is offered here as a tentative hypothesis.

One critic has called *Saving Private Ryan* a "secular Jeremiad" – a term derived from the Old Testament prophet Jeremiah – describing the film as a call to corrective action, a call to the community to return to its foundational principles.[29] Conceived as a form of secular Jeremiad, the film can be seen to serve a dual function for American culture: it both acknowledges the crisis brought on by Vietnam and the dissolution of the covenant between the state and its people, while also offering audiences a "way home" to a mythic America, reaffirming American national identity after the crisis of Vietnam. The affirmation by Ryan's wife and daughters at the end of the film directs us away from an impression of random and overwhelming loss. Instead, the final scene reestablishes a covenant with the past, and constructs the memory of

World War II, reinforced by the memory of the Holocaust, as a resource for American national identity after Vietnam.

Notes

1   For a discussion of the concept of "genre memory," see Gary Saul Morson and Caryl Emerson, *Mikhail Bakhtin: The Creation of a Prosaics* (Stanford, CA: Stanford University Press, 1990): 290–2.

2   André Bazin, *What Is Cinema?*, trans. Hugh Gray (Berkeley and Los Angeles: University of California Press, 1967): vol. 1: 31–3. This translation by David Forgacs, *Rome Open City* (London: British Film Institute, 2000): 23.

3   Thomas Doherty, *Cineaste*, 24(1): 68–71.

4   For a powerful reading of the effects of the D-Day landing sequence on World War II veterans, see Janet Walker, "The Vicissitudes of Traumatic Memory and the Postmodern History Film," in E. Ann Kaplan and Ban Wang, eds., *Trauma and Cinema: Cross Cultural Explorations* (Hong Kong: Hong Kong University Press, 2004): 123–44.

5   See J. David Slocum, "Cinema and the Civilizing Process: Rethinking Violence in the World War II Combat Film," *Cinema Journal* 44(3) (2005): 35–63.

6   A. Susan Owen, "Memory, War, and American Identity: *Saving Private Ryan* as Cinematic Jeremiad," *Critical Studies in Media Communication* 19(3) (September 2002): 263.

7   Kaplan and Ban Wang, *Trauma and Cinema*. See especially Kaplan, "Traumatic Contact Zones and Embodied Translators": 45–64.

8   Alison Griffiths, " 'Shivers Down Your Spine': Panoramas and the Origins of the Cinematic Reenactment," *Screen* 44(1) (2003): 11.

9   Ibid.: 16.

10   Quoted in ibid.: 19.

11   Richard Slotkin, *Regeneration Through Violence* (Middletown, CT: Wesleyan University Press, 1973).

12   Bakhtin, in Morson and Emerson, *Mikhail Bakhtin*. See also Robert Burgoyne, *Film Nation: Hollywood Looks at U.S. History* (Minneapolis: University of Minnesota Press, 1997): 7–9.

13   Peter Ehrenhaus, "Why We Fought: Holocaust Memory in Spielberg's *Saving Private Ryan*," *Critical Studies in Media Communication* 18(3) (2001): 323. Ehrenhaus quotes Christopher Caldwell in *Commentary*, October 1998: 50.

14   The "reillusionment" of America is a phrase used by M. Wallace in *Mickey Mouse History and Other Essays on American Memory* (Philadelphia, PA: Temple University Press, 1996).

15   Ehrenhaus, "Why We Fought: Holocaust Memory": 322.

16 The dualism of duty and emotion is especially prominent in the epic film. Leon Hunt explores this theme in detail in "What Are Big Boys Made Of? *Spartacus, El Cid,* and the Male Epic," in Pat Kirkham and Janet Thumin, eds., *You Tarzan: Masculinity, Movies and Men* (London: Lawrence & Wishart, reprinted New York: St. Martin's Press, 1993): 65–83.

17 Merrill D. Peterson, *Lincoln in American Memory* (New York: Oxford University Press, 1994): 244, 246. Quoted in Al Auster, "Saving Private Ryan and American Triumphalism," in Robert Eberwein, ed., *The War Film* (New Brunswick, NJ: Rutgers University Press, 2005): 205–13.

18 Sacvan Bercovitch, *The American Jeremiad* (Madison: University of Wisconsin Press, 1978): 176.

19 Ehrenhaus, "Why We Fought": 332.

20 Steve Neale, "Aspects of Ideology and Narrative Form in the American War Film," *Screen*, 32(1) (Spring 1991): 35–57.

21 Dana Polan, "Auteurism and War-teurism: Terence Malick's War Movie," in Eberwein, *The War Film*, p. 60.

22 Ehrenhaus, "Why We Fought": 323.

23 Ibid.: 324.

24 Ibid.: 335.

25 See Owen, "Memory, War, and American Identity": 263.

26 M. Johnson, "Jones Makes Impact in 'Heaven': A Heaven and Earth with Muted Force, *Hartford Courant*, p. B1. Quoted in Owen, "Memory, War, and American Identity": 256.

27 Pierre Sorlin, "Cinema and the Memory of the Great War," in Michael Paris, ed., *The First World War and Popular Cinema* (New Brunswick, NJ: Rutgers University Press, 2000).

28 Polan, "Auteurism and War-teurism": 56.

29 Owen, "Memory, War, and American Identity": 249–82.

CHAPTER 3

THE EPIC FILM: *GLADIATOR* AND *SPARTACUS*

The spectacular critical and commercial success of *Gladiator*, a success that has led to a number of new productions of epic films whose setting is the ancient world, is a striking example of the resiliency of genre forms, their ability, in the words of Mikhail Bakhtin, to "remember the past, while making their resources available to the present." Genres function as "organs of memory" for particular cultures, Bakhtin writes, providing crystallized forms of social and cultural memory that embody the worldviews of the periods in which they originated, while carrying with them "the layered record of their changing use." Genres "resume past usage . . . and redefine present experience in an additional way."[1] As a film that both rehearses and revises the epic tradition, *Gladiator* provides an opportunity to consider the way genre films both recall past usages and respond to the present in a new way. The complex dialogue that *Gladiator* sets up with the epic tradition is particularly visible in its reworking of specific scenes from *Spartacus*, a film that has been associated, despite its complicated production and reception history, with the emancipatory politics of the 1960s. The historical signals and cultural values associated with *Spartacus* interpenetrate and affect the construction of new images in *Gladiator*, illustrating the ways in which memories of history and nation are called forth and reconfigured as they are adapted to a new context.

One writer has said that "true film epics can only be made at a time when a country's national myths are still believed – or when a nation feels itself slipping into decline, which produces a spate of nostalgic evocations of those myths."[2] Usually associated with spectacle, monumentality, and lavish *mise en scène*, the epic mode of representation has recently been critically reevaluated as a distilled expression of ideals, anxieties, and conflicts in national self-definition.[3] Gilles Deleuze provides an interesting perspective on the American film that seems to have a special salience for understanding the attractions of the epic:

> the American cinema constantly shoots and reshoots a single fundamental film, which is the birth of a nation-civilization . . . it and it alone is the whole of history, the germinating stock from which each nation-civilization detaches itself as an organism, each prefiguring America . . . a strong ethical judgment must condemn the injustice of "things," bring compassion, herald the new civilization on the march, in short, constantly rediscover America.[4]

The connection Deleuze draws between the American cinema and the drive to narrate the birth of the nation-civilization rings especially true for the tradition of the Roman epic, for Hollywood films set in ancient Rome have become an important part of the historical capital of modern US culture.

As Maria Wyke explains in *Projecting the Past*, Hollywood's Roman history films are in many ways an extension of a long tradition of borrowing from the Roman past in order to crystallize and critique aspects of American national identity. From the founding years of the nation-state, the imagery of ancient Rome was deployed to link the civic ideals of the fledgling nation to the classical past with its ready-made connotations of democracy, liberty, and nobility. George Washington, for example, was frequently pictured in Roman garb, and the architecture of Washington, DC was modeled on the Roman Forum. However, Rome was also identified with decadence and opulence, and many early commentators at various points compared the likely fate of the United States to the ultimate fate of the Roman Empire. Hollywood films set in Rome often exploited the ambiguities and contradictions associated with ancient Rome as a site of both ideal civic virtue and decadent excess and imperial domination to express the social iniquities within the United States itself. In drawing on the ancient Roman past to forge images of the American nation, however, Hollywood filmmakers also were able to showcase the cinema's own technological prowess. Ancient Rome became a privileged site for the spectacular display of the technology of cinema. As Michael Wood writes, Hollywood's histories of Rome became "a huge, many-faceted metaphor for Hollywood itself."[5] The depiction of ancient Rome on screen came to stand for Hollywood's own glamour, grandeur, and aesthetic innovation. In the words of Wyke:

> The projection of ancient Rome on screen has functioned not only as a mechanism for the display or interrogation of national identities but also, and often in contradiction, as a mechanism for the display of cinema itself – its technical capacities and its cultural value . . . Ancient Rome has been constantly reinvented to suit new technologies for its cinematic narration and new historical contexts for the interpretation of the Roman past in the present.[6]

Gladiator provides a striking example of the ways in which the Roman epic serves as a mechanism for the display of new technologies of cinema. With its computer-generated main sets of the Colosseum and the Roman Forum and its computer-enhanced battle and combat scenes, *Gladiator* has a visual depth and apparent authenticity that is unsurpassed. Its vivid resurrection of the ancient world manages to make that world seem both familiar and deeply other. Drawing on familiar imagery from paintings, earlier films, and architectural models, *Gladiator* provides a high-tech, computer-generated picture of the Roman past that simultaneously celebrates and critiques the theatrical iconography of imperial power. For example, in a striking analysis of the computer-assisted architectural design and mass crowd scenes of *Gladiator*, Arthur J. Pomeroy details the film's use of visual ideas from Leni Riefenstahl's *Triumph of the Will*, particularly in the spectacular scene of Commodus' entry into Rome. Here, the camera's descent from the clouds, the passage through the crowd, and Commodus' arrival at the steps of the Senate to be greeted by a little girl with a bouquet of flowers echo scenes from Riefenstahl's film. The massed population of Romans greeting Commodus as he stands atop the Senate steps is a direct reference to the massed soldiers of *Triumph of the Will*. Moreover, the film's depiction of the Roman Forum, Pomeroy points out, with its Senate at one end and the Colosseum at the other, flanked by massive buildings and columns, is closer to the planned architecture of "Germania," Hitler's grandiose vision for a new Berlin, than it is to the historic Roman Forum.[7] The technology of cinema is here used to evoke the Roman past in a way that echoes the imagery associated with the Third Reich. In its use of quotations from *Triumph of the Will*, *Gladiator* links technology and spectacle in a way that offers a distinctive historiography, one that underlines the Roman epic as a layered record, and as a vehicle for shaping and carrying social and historical experience from one generation to another. The film clearly "remembers the past," including the ways Rome has been understood and interpreted in other periods, strikingly illustrating the effect that Bakhtin calls "double voicing."

The technological prowess that is such a distinctive feature of the Hollywood Roman epic is part of the heritage of the epic film, an aspect of its genre memory. From the first epics such as *Cabiria* and *Intolerance*, the epic film has been defined by colossal sets and innovative photographic effects. For Deleuze, however, the feature that is most significant in the epic is not its monumental forms but rather its ethical, critical vision, its transformative power, its ability to transfigure the accomplishments of the past. In his lucid analysis of the epic film, Deleuze suggests that the American epic film articulates a particularly strong and coherent conception of what he calls "universal history," bringing together three of the most important aspects of history as seen by the nineteenth century. Drawing on Nietzsche's analysis of German nineteenth-century historiography, Deleuze defines these three aspects as monumental history, antiquarian history, and critical or ethical history. Monumental history concerns the physical, the architectural, and the natural milieu; the desert and the sea, the pyramids and the temples, Cleopatra's barge and the walled city of Troy. Monumental history, he writes, tends toward the universal, favoring "analogies or parallels between one civilization and another: the great moments of humanity communicate "via the peaks." In film, monumental history, history via analogy, has its greatest embodiment in D. W. Griffith's *Intolerance*, for it compares four different civilizations not sequentially but in an alternating montage, making comparisons at an ever-increasing tempo. Antiquarian history, on the other hand, concerns itself with the intimate customs and accoutrements of the historical past, the tapestries, the fabrics, the weapons and tools, but also the typical ritualized forms of the era, the duels and gladiator contests, the chariot races and tournaments; these are the signs of the "actualization of the epoch." Here Deleuze cites *Samson and Delilah*, for its concentration on the "peaks of colour" given in the fabric of the tunics Samson steals, or the machinery in *The Land of the Pharaohs* in which Howard Hawks seems mainly interested in depicting the "extraordinary new machine" for mixing sand and stone that will hermetically seal the Pharaoh's tomb. Finally, and most importantly, Deleuze writes that critical or ethical history is necessary to bring these two types together, for it "measures and organizes them both." The ancient past must be made to disclose the "ferments of decadence and the germs of new life . . . the orgy and the sign of the cross, the omnipotence of the rich and the misery of the poor." A strong ethical judgment must "herald the new civilization on the march." The analogical, parallelist conception that organizes the epic constitutes, for Deleuze, its "implicit conception of history."[8]

This ethical–critical aspect of history is centrifugally organized around the epic hero, whose name often provides the title of the film. Here Deleuze makes a suggestive distinction between pastoral epics, such as Westerns, in which there is an "equivalence of the soul and the world, of the hero and the milieu," where the hero does not so much change or alter the milieu as reestablish it, "as one might re-make a road," and the epic film organized around an ethical–critical vision, in which the hero is not content to reestablish the threatened order, and where the ethical vision alters the milieu. This type of film, Deleuze writes, is organized in the form of a spiral, rather than a circle; the situation of

FIGURE 3.1 The patrician Crassus (Laurence Olivier), lord of all he surveys – with certain exceptions. *Spartacus* (1960) [Universal International Pictures/Photofest]

arrival differs from the situation of departure.[9] The tension between these two types of epic form is condensed in the figure of the epic hero, who is often shown as divided between the pastoral and the ethical.

In a perceptive essay, Leon Hunt describes the contradictory aspects of the ideal forms of masculinity that are constructed in the epic film: "The films invest in two agendas, one based on heroism, duty, law, death, and one based on emotions, tears, love and desire. It is the theme of sacrifice which unites them." The epic's scenes of male sacrifice often create a "profoundly melodramatic experience, emotional, hysterical, over-whelming."[10] In the pages that follow, I will consider the way the epic film articulates an imaginary field in which issues of nation, masculinity, and history are set in bold relief. By comparing three closely related scenes from *Spartacus* and *Gladiator*, I will also explore the way genre forms impose their own historical perspectives and systems of value on individual texts.

Universal History

The opening voice-over narration of *Spartacus* foregrounds the ethical vision of the epic film, describing Rome as a republic "that lay fatally stricken with a disease called human slavery," and describing Spartacus as a "proud, rebellious son dreaming of the death of slavery, 2000 years before it finally would die." Although the use of voice-over narrations and epigraphs is a convention in epic cinema, in *Spartacus* we find its emblematic expression. The organic metaphors that dominate the narration – the birth of Christianity, the diseased condition of Rome, and the final death of slavery in America – evoke the motif of the body as an emblem of nation, a body that suffers from decay and disease, but that also contains the germs of new life, a regeneration that Spartacus sets in motion a full century before the "birth" of Christianity. Even prior to the voice-over, however, the credit sequence of the film had initiated the motif of decline and decay. In a stunning sequence designed by Saul Bass, we view a series of images of marble busts and sculptures, a kind of museum-memory of ancient Rome – the Rome of patrician senators and omnipotent Caesars, of slaves with manacled hands and open-palmed gestures – animated through dramatic dissolves and superimpositions. Each of these marble forms iconically represents one of the main characters – manacled hands for Spartacus, a hand with a pitcher of water representing Varinia, who will become Spartacus' woman and the mother of his son, a hand holding a bird for Antoninus, the "singer of songs," and other images for the Roman general Crassus and the slave-trader, Batiatus. But the last image, a wild-eyed and grotesque-looking bust of a laurelled emperor, crumbles and breaks apart as if under pressure from within. Thus by the time the character Spartacus is introduced, the film has established the motifs of Rome as a decadent nation, a sick organism, and has pointed to the eventual emergence of new life in a healthy nation-civilization two thousand years later. A universal history has been traced, and its teleological resolution discovered; Spartacus emerges into the camera's view already established as the agent of this universal history.

Shown in full shot wielding a pickax, Spartacus exhibits a bronzed, sweating muscularity, a physical power and muscular tonicity that provides an immediate contrast with the motifs of disease and death established in the voice-over and credit sequence. But the focus on his physical strength quickly shifts to another code of epic symbolism. As he strains to carry a load of rocks up a ridge, a fellow slave collapses under his load. Spartacus throws down his burden and immediately goes to help him. Roman punishment ensues, and by the end of the sequence, Spartacus is tied to a boulder, arms spread, crucified. Nevertheless, the health of the future nation-civilization is embodied in him, for in this highly iconographic moment the film recalls the epic films of the past with their formulaic conflict of Roman versus Christian. Even though the film's producer, director, and writer had insisted on distinguishing the film from the typical Christian focus of 1950s epics – the filmmakers called it the "thinking man's epic" – the memory of earlier epic films informs and colors its narrative message.

The opening of *Gladiator* emits a very different set of messages, which nevertheless converge in the hints of sacrifice that surround the presentation of the hero. Although the film evokes the epic tradition, it initially seems to draw different lessons from the ancient past. Like the Hollywood Roman epics of the 1950s and 1960s, *Gladiator* treats ancient Rome as a prefiguration of America. And like *Spartacus*, the film establishes a connection between Rome and America from the opening moments of the film, making an explicit comparison between the imperial power of Rome and the global reach of Hollywood. *Gladiator* begins in a way that underlines Michael Wood's point about Rome serving as a metaphor for the power and reach of Hollywood itself. In colors of dark gold and black, the Universal Studios logo spins into view to inaugurate the film. A glowing, slowly spinning globe, the image is set against a black celestial background, with the globe turning so as to emphasize first Africa and Europe, then North and South America.

The written inscription "Universal" orbits out from behind the globe to engirdle it. In the next set of images, a smoky, dull red background is seen, and another inscription appears stating that "At the height of its power, the Roman Empire was vast, stretching from the deserts of Africa to the borders of Northern England. Over one-quarter of the world's population lived and died under the rule of the Caesars . . . Just one final stronghold stands in the way of Roman victory and the promise of peace throughout the empire." The Universal logo sequence and the historical epigraph form a striking parallel construction: Hollywood and Rome both encircle the world; one empire seamlessly flowing into the other.

Following *Gladiator's* opening invocation of the Empire's reach, the film begins quietly. A tracking shot follows a man walking through a golden wheat field with his hand held out, grazing the tops of the wheat stalks. A haunting, mournful voice sings over these images, as the distant sound of children's laughter and the sound of wind carries the shot along. Suddenly, we cut to a frontal shot of Maximus, in a contemplative pose, a shot that has a cold, blue, and smoky look to it, creating a contrast with the warm hues of the wheat field in the earlier tracking shot. A Spanish guitar is heard on the soundtrack. Maximus is dressed for battle, and his face is grimy, unshaven, and resolute.

In this opening sequence, Maximus is associated with the natural world of wheat fields and children's' voices, with the earth that he rubs into his hands and the bird that lands near him. But he is also associated with the imagery of war, the smoke and ash and the song of mourning that we hear on the soundtrack. In this version of the Roman epic, however, the Empire is associated not with sickness and death, but with the promise of peace; far from the "fatally stricken," diseased Rome of *Spartacus*, the Roman Empire is here one victory away from attaining "peace throughout the Empire." And from the opening moments of the film, Maximus is defined as the agent of this historical process. Although he is portrayed in a static portraiture shot, with a thoughtful, premonitory expression on his face, the residue of tradition clings to the figure of Maximus: the epic past is crystallized in his powerful build, in his commanding gaze, and in his evident stature in the narrative world, signified by the framing, cutting, and camera movement with which he is introduced.

Epic films provide a "layered record," recalling past usages even as they respond to the present in new ways. The epic form, in keeping with Bakhtin's understanding of genre memory, imposes its own historical perspectives and systems of value even when a film employs genre codes in a nontraditional manner. An example of this can be found in *Gladiator*. A few moments after the opening portrait shots of Maximus, the music changes to the stirring main theme of the film; the pensive opening glimpses of the private Maximus give way to a series of tracking shots of the character walking through a file of soldiers, all of whom rise to greet him, looking fully at him with respect and even love, a few of whom he touches in passing as he touched the stalks of wheat in the opening shot. The extraordinary tracking shots of Maximus moving among his legions, his dog running alongside him, are overpowering, flooding the screen with emotion. With the camera detailing the wide-eyed responses of his soldiers as he moves among them, and detailing the exceptional feeling visible on the face of Marcus Aurelius as he watches Maximus from on high, the scene draws equally on the iconography of empire and on the iconography of the biblical epic, condensing both in the figure of Maximus. In these opening shots, Maximus, like Spartacus, is defined as the agent of a universal history whose outline contains sacred and secular motifs, revealed in crystallized form in the epic Roman past.

But another message can be sensed in the opening as well, a message that has found its way into certain cultural responses to the film, and that I would like to highlight here as a motif that might lead to another type of reading. What is unusual about the logo, epigraph, and opening sequence in *Gladiator* is the somber, melancholy mood that the opening communicates, as if the film were a collective commemoration ritual, the recalling of an ancient past not in order to express a triumphal communication with the Roman empire via the peaks, but rather to express a contemporary sense of foreboding and crisis. *Gladiator*, released in the year 2000, seems to foreshadow the crisis of national identity and modern social structures catalyzed by the events of 9/11.

The figure of Maximus, and the film itself, have been inscribed in American culture in a particularly complex and resonant way. Maximus, for example, became a popular figure in body art in the immediate aftermath of 9/11, with the figure of the gladiator assuming a particular value as an icon of honor and mourning. The imagery associated with *Gladiator*, integrated into the shield and battalion imagery of firefighters, became a favored way of memorializing fallen firefighters, and the slogan, "Strength and Honor" featured in the film became a popular inscription in tattoos.[11] A more complete indexing of borrowed and repurposed imagery from the film would undoubtedly reveal an extensive array of narratives and discourses in which the film has been inscribed. What I wish to emphasize here is one of the ways that *Gladiator* has been connected to a powerful and particular moment of national anxiety and trauma, to a changing concept of nation, and to surprising acts of solidarity with the past. The relationship between commemoration, collective mourning, and body modification, including tattooing and scarification, circulating within the cultural responses to *Gladiator*, suggests that the imagery and narrative messages of the contemporary epic are open to appropriation in ways that are not limited by nationalistic or imperialistic expressions, but rather may serve different, vernacular needs.

Writing the Body

The extensive literature on tattooing and scarification emphasizes its connection to liminal moments of social and historical crisis; the popularity of tattooing peaks during periods of cultural, social, and religious upheaval. In some cultures, tattoos are regarded as magical, an invocation against death and an expression of the desire for rebirth, a theme that is patently present in the imagery popular in tattoos seen after 9/11. Much of the commentary on tattoos after 9/11 describes them as a form of solace, as "medicinal," and as "a public declaration of loss, defiance, and survival," themes that link them explicitly to blood rituals of inclusion and community, to the idea of passage through ordeal, to a kind of "writing on the body by experience," and to remembrance and commemoration.[12] Here, the practice of tattooing speaks to an alternative understanding of being in history. As Kim Hewitt writes, tattoos and body scarification are "acts that asked to be witnessed."[13]

The popularity of *Gladiator* as a source of imagery for tattoos – one of the best known ink parlors in New York is named "Maximus Tattoos" – brings into relief certain aspects of the film that have not yet been explored in the critical literature. Considered in terms of this kind of vernacular recoding, the film's narrative takes on a different coloration than that described by many critical theorists, one of blood ritual and commemoration, of identities constructed outside the dominant discourse. The vernacular response to the film, with its emphasis on the physical, somatic re-experiencing of loss and remembrance, suggests that for some audiences its narrative patterning and imagery are deeply interwoven with a sense of the physical, corporeal body.

In a well-known essay, Paul Willeman writes about the voyeuristic pleasure involved in viewing the male figure in film, and describes the way certain film genres typically display the male body: "The viewer's experience is predicated on the pleasure of seeing the male 'exist' (that is, walk, move, ride, fight) in or through cityscapes, landscapes, or more abstractedly, history. And on the unquiet pleasure of seeing the male mutilated . . . and restored through violent brutality."[14] The spectacle of the male figure riding, fighting, or moving "through history" is of course the keystone of the epic cinema, along with the violent brutality that finds the male hero first mutilated and then symbolically restored.[15] But as *Spartacus* and *Gladiator* make clear, the epic film also crystallizes broader cultural themes that coalesce around the performance of masculinity as an emblematic expression of national imaginings. The epic film hero embodies not just an archaic, nostalgic ideal of heroism shadowed by tones of sacrifice and loss, but rather displays in somatic form competing visions of historical identity, often serving as the distilled expression of a national narrative in the process of being redefined.

Spartacus is a film that was made at the end of one of the most repressive, fearful periods in American history, and there are obvious parallels throughout the film to the political climate of the 1950s. The Civil Rights Movement, the McCarthy hearings, the Women's Movement, Zionism, are plainly visible subtexts of the film. The extensive literature on the production and reception history of the film reveals that *Spartacus* was subject to a range of competing cultural agendas. Throughout the production process, the screenwriter, Dalton Trumbo, the producer and star, Kirk Douglas, the novelist Howard Fast, and the director Stanley Kubrick struggled over contradictory ideas about Spartacus' motivations, character, and leadership.[16] When the film was released, it was picketed by the Legion of Decency, scrutinized for communist messages, and celebrated by the mainstream press. Audiences of the time saw Spartacus through various lenses, as a left-wing militant, as a "Cold-War warrior" demonstrating "man's eternal desire for freedom," and as a sacrificial, Christ-like figure whose aspirations were "assimilated to the alternative, divinely blessed values of democratic America." The controversy over its political message and its legitimacy as an expression of national aspirations wasn't stilled until the newly elected John F. Kennedy crossed a picket line set up by anti-communist organizers to attend the film.[17]

Similarly, many contemporary critics understand the climactic scenes of spectacle in *Gladiator* in terms of a direct projection of dominant political values. Characterizing the film in terms of the "hegemonic technology of sublime spectacle" or as the "techno-euphoric reign of aestheticized spectacles of empire," writers such as Rob Wilson and Brian White equate *Gladiator* with the strategies and values of the dominant political culture, specifically the projection of US cultural and military hegemony across the globe. Emphasizing parallels between its portrayal of Imperial Rome and the imperial globalization of the American political, cultural, and military orders, Wilson characterizes *Gladiator* as the "legitimation of the imperial machine."[18] The message communicated by the film, in this reading, is a message concerning new forms of imperialism characterized as "soft hegemony," or "imperial humanitarianism," expressed through Maximus' identification with subaltern groups, the slaves and gladiators from Gaul, Africa, Germania, and Spain, including the Germanic tribes that he defeats in the opening sequences of the film. But these "soft" messages, in this view, are contained within an overarching discourse of domination and imperialism, as the technological and cultural superiority of the dominant culture is happily reaffirmed in sublime orchestrations of unprecedented visual spectacle. Wilson writes that "*Gladiator* helps to make this amorphous Empire palpable as a global structure of feeling. The movie . . . secures consent to its military machine not so much via domination and plunder as via aesthetic ratification, mediated trauma, and modes of civilian awe."[19]

Spectacle, however, is only one component of the epic text; by emphasizing what Deleuze calls the "monumental" aspect of epic form, these writers ignore the ethical–critical register of the epic, which is also primarily expressed through the body of the epic hero. Deleuze argues that the epic text synthesizes the monumental, the antiquarian, and the ethical–critical registers of the epic text in a fully coherent form, an emphasis that highlights the thematic range and complexity of the epic. As writers such as Wyke, Monica Cyrino, and Mark Jancovich point out, competing concepts of national identity and historical meaning are often consolidated and expressed in epic form.[20] These messages coalesce in many cases around the body of the epic hero. The pleasure of watching the male "exist," or "move through history," in Willeman's words, frequently extends to the theme of collective emergence, the founding of a nation or a people in films such as *Gladiator*, *Spartacus*, *The Ten Commandments*, and *El Cid*.[21] Epic films emphasize not only the somatic authority of the epic hero, but also the physical, creaturely body, seen in the masses of slaves and subalterns, in the great crowds of the marginal and excluded, in the tribes of nomads and congeries of exiles that populate the epic film. The ethical and moral message of these films seems to be centered in the depiction of "bare life," understood as the repository of collective identity, moral gravity, and historical change.[22] In films such as *Spartacus* and *Gladiator*, and in many other epic films, the epic hero gains the authority, the mandate to complete his quest only after becoming one with the multitude, falling into slavery, becoming a nomad, drawing from the multitude a heightened sense of purpose and nobility.

When the body displayed on the screen is the body of a male slave, a complex set of historical and symbolic messages emerge, messages that have not yet been considered in discussions of masculinity in epic films. In *Spartacus* and in *Gladiator*, the body of the male slave becomes a kind of document, on which questions of ownership, authorship, and history are traced and retraced, and in which the familiar narratives of honor, emotion, and sacrifice become fraught and complicated by questions of agency and collective purpose. The translation of the body of the male slave into the person of the epic hero highlights the performative aspect of masculinity in the epic cinema, a performance that must resolve symbolic contradictions between slavery and masculinity, between individual subordination and collective agency.

As Hunt has shown, the ultimate form of empowerment in the male epic is the gesture of self-sacrifice. The male epic invests in competing agendas that emphasize tensions between duty and love, destiny and emotion, patriarchal obligation and tender feelings. This tension is resolved only in the trope of male sacrifice, he writes, for only in the sacrificial gesture can the emotions of vulnerability and love merge with the requirements of a heroic destiny. In the case of the male slave, however, self-sacrifice takes on an additional meaning – here the theme of sacrifice becomes a form of self-authorship, the slave asserting mastery over his own body, a gesture that gives the body a poetic, metaphoric meaning.

In *Spartacus*, the motif of male sacrifice is directly tied to the issue of race and racial slavery, a reference that gives contemporary resonance to the film's relentless depiction of Rome as a civilization based on slavery. Race emerges in a powerful way in the gladiator fight between Spartacus and Draba, the black gladiator that Spartacus had attempted to befriend. Draba earlier had refused Spartacus' friendly overtures because, as he says, "You don't want to know my name, I don't want to know your name . . . Gladiators don't make friends. If we're ever matched in the arena together, I'll have to kill you." When the moment of truth arrives, however, Draba refuses to kill Spartacus, and chooses to sacrifice himself instead.

The sequence of Draba and Spartacus in the ring has been extensively analyzed as a critique of spectacle and the dehumanizing agenda of the arena. As Ina Rae Hark writes, the gladiators were trained to enact on each other the domination the Romans exerted over them; masculine subjectivity is defined here only through the ability to dominate others. But what sets the Romans apart from the gladiators, in her reading, is the power of the gaze; even though the gladiators are constructed as

FIGURE 3.2 Spartacus (Kirk Douglas) and Draba (Woody Strode), forced to fight "to the death," embody the violent testing that is at the heart of the male epic. *Spartacus* (1960) [Universal International Pictures/Photofest]

hypermasculine, they remain objects of spectacle, passive vessels for the pleasure of the Romans: "the permission to become a spectator demarcates the master from the slave . . . Rome enforces power by making spectacles of those it dominates."[23] The slave is excluded from these games of mastery, for the gladiator-slave, even when he dominates other gladiators, merely mirrors Roman power, reenacting the power Rome exerts over all the gladiator-slaves. Draba, however, refuses his assigned role. When Draba and Spartacus fight, it ends with Spartacus under Draba's spear, at his mercy. Draba looks to Crassus, who gives the thumbs-down sign. In an intense scene of self-scrutiny, Draba looks again at Spartacus, turns toward the watching Romans, and hurls his trident at the box

FIGURE 3.3 Draba (Woody Strode) at a moment of decision. Sparing Spartacus (Kirk Douglas), he decides to sacrifice himself, leaping onto the parapet and inspiring the slave rebellion that follows. *Spartacus* (1960) [Universal International Pictures/Photofest]

where Crassus sits. He then scales the high wall to attack the senator sitting above. Crassus unsheathes his dagger and slits Draba's neck, his blood splattering Crassus' face.

In analyzing the scene as a commentary on spectacle and dehumanization, Hark notes that the trident that Draba throws at Crassus is aimed at the camera, as if our cinematic gaze were assimilated to that of the Romans. Moreover, the refusal of Draba to watch an earlier fight, and the several barriers to vision that are imposed on our gaze throughout, suggest that to view the spectacle is to be complicit in it. But this analysis ignores the racial content of the scene, a key component of the film's overall message of freedom and brotherhood. Draba is played by the actor Woody Strode, who was well known for his earlier role in the anti-rascist film *Sergeant Rutledge*; Draba's self-sacrifice, his gesture of mastery over his own body and his own fate, his self-authorship, bring into relief the powerful resonance that *Spartacus* finds in the slave rebellion as a prefiguration of the American national story.[24]

Although ancient Rome and Greece were slave societies, Roman slavery was not racialized, but was based instead on the enslavement of foreigners. Romans had the absolute right not to be slaves of other Romans: a "bond of freedom shared by male Roman citizens at all levels of wealth was shored up by the enslavement of foreigners . . . The presence of a substantial number of slaves in Roman society defined free citizens, even if they were poor, as superior."[25] Because of this, a paradoxical situation arose that M. I. Finley describes as "the advance, hand in hand, of freedom and slavery."[26] For the Romans to be free meant that a substantial portion of the external population had to be enslaved. As the number of free Romans increased, a greater and greater number of foreign lands had to be conquered. Freedom and slavery, as Finley says, advanced "hand in hand."

American freedom and slavery revolved around a similar paradox. As Nathan Huggins writes, "Freedom among the white servant classes and lower orders had meaning precisely because of slavery. Racial slavery created among white men a kind of equality (in freedom) and a common bond which could be made to take precedence over all other interests . . . American freedom finds its meaning in American slavery."[27] Viewed from this perspective, the scene featuring Draba's sacrifice takes on a specifically national, allegorical meaning. The black gladiator Draba leaps onto the parapet as if he were leaping onto the balcony of history to remind us of the legacy of slavery, and the way it is bound to our idealized conceptions of freedom, Roman and American. He confronts both Crassus and the film's spectator. The film suggests here that slavery and race are at the center of US history, as slavery was at the center of the history of Rome. The film also establishes in Spartacus an obligation; as Draba's sacrifice comes to signify a historical debt, it assumes the status of a message that should not so much be read as lived.

This point is reinforced in the scene that immediately follows. Draba's body has been strung up in the slave-gladiators' quarters, hung upside down, arms extended in a kind of inverted crucifixion. As the gladiators somberly walk down the stone stairs into their gloomy quarters, the body of Draba hangs in the foreground as a reminder of what will happen to them if they disobey. But as the gladiators file down the stairs, the camera frames each of them through the narrow gap between Draba's calves, emphasizing the meaning of Draba's sacrifice, as if Draba's body were the gate or the portal through which they must pass to become free men.

In *Gladiator*, the relationship of Maximus and Juba, the African gladiator who heals Maximus' wounded arm, rehearses the pairing of Spartacus and Draba, but converts it to a very different message. After being terribly wounded in his struggle with the Roman execution squad, Maximus follows Juba's instruction to let maggots eat away the infected flesh; Juba then embeds the wound with healing paste. Juba becomes something like a spiritual healer for Maximus as well, as they talk about their families and the afterlife. Like the actor Woody Strode, Djimon Hounsou brings to the role of Juba an antiracist screen persona; he had earlier played the role of Cinque, leader of the slave rebellion in *Amistad*. With intertextual echoes of Cinque and Draba augmenting the character's largely symbolic role, Juba becomes a kind of textual amplifier, reinforcing the film's signals of epic renewal and emergence, providing an ethical–critical memory link to the parallel historical text that shapes the film's vision of the past.

From this point forward, the film weaves together the stories of Maximus and Juba, a device that is reflected in the interweaving of musical styles in the film's soundtrack, which increasingly features African and Asian motifs. In the black–white pairing of Maximus and Juba, the traditional epic themes – the emergence of a people, the birth of a nation, the fulfillment of a heroic destiny – are here rewritten to express a story of emergence in which black and white are connected by a central thread. Chained together in the ring in one early scene, Maximus and Juba must fight as one in order to survive. Shadowing each other's movements, the two gladiators are virtuosos, performing a spectacular, choreographic duet in which they devastate their opponents, devise a new weapon from the chain that binds them, and arouse the crowd to frenzy.

FIGURE 3.4 Chained together in the ring, Maximus (Russell Crowe) and Juba (Djimon Honsou) replay the black–white pairing of Spartacus and Draba, but instead of fighting each other, they perform as a virtuoso pair. *Gladiator* (2000) [DreamWorks SKG/Photofest]

Unlike *Spartacus*, however, *Gladiator* seems to emphasize what Friedrich Nietzsche calls the "will to power" expressed in agonistic battle, the "visual stimulation of watching muscular bodies in vigorous exertion, defying death and injury."[28] Maximus theatrically penetrates the bodies of his antagonists, burying two swords in the chest of one combatant, and then removing them to whack his head off with an unforgettable flourish. He emerges from darkness to destroy opponents that are depersonalized, variously outfitted in bull's-head helmets, armored from head to toe, or outfitted with other odd and monstrous accoutrements. He battles an assortment of combatants disguised as chthonic monsters. And in a scene that directly quotes and then revises Draba's sacrifice in *Spartacus*, Maximus, after devastating scores of combatants, hurls his sword at the box where the slave-owner Proximo sits. The camera, as in *Spartacus*, is positioned so that the sword seems to be aimed directly at it. Maximus then berates the audience, demanding "Are you not entertained? Isn't this what you came for? Are you not entertained?" Where *Spartacus* used this gesture to suggest the spectator's own complicity in dehumanization and violence, *Gladiator* converts the scene into the expression of a different message. As the camera arches upward, the music swells, and the crowd begins chanting Maximus' nickname, "Spaniard! Spaniard! Spaniard!," resolving the scene into an expression of celebratory triumph. Here, *Gladiator* evokes *Spartacus* but imbues it, as Bakhtin might say, with a very different "social accent."

The theme of violence as a socially redemptive act, a theme that hinges on recoding the punitive agency of martial combat into the ennobling rhetoric of blood myths, evokes Richard Slotkin's analysis of the theme of "regeneration through violence" in American literature of the frontier period.[29] But unlike Slotkin's isolated frontier hunter, who roamed freely over the land dominating and subduing nature, purified by acts of violence, the hero of *Gladiator* is burdened with a more complicated agenda: he must somehow connect the violence, the blood rhetoric of the gladiatorial ring, with the idealized vision of Roman *civitas* articulated by Marcus Aurelius early in the film as the "dream" of Rome. *Gladiator* thus responds to *Spartacus* in a paradoxical fashion by centering on the agonistic duels that are absent from the earlier film. Whereas *Spartacus* renounces the arena as a privileged site for the performance of masculine agency, *Gladiator* moves the arena to the center of its consideration of the meaning and importance of performative masculinity for epic cinema.

The punitive agency that dominates the scenes of gladiatorial combat in *Gladiator*, scenes that set this film apart from epics such as *Spartacus* and *Ben Hur*, can be seen as serving a national mythology that is quite different from that of *Spartacus*, invoking a form of blood rhetoric in defense of a concept of nation that the film suggests reaches back to the Rome of Marcus Aurelius. Unlike older Hollywood Roman films, including *Spartacus*, there is no Christological alternative in *Gladiator*; where older epics often had the fall of the Roman Empire and the advent of Christianity as their teleological point of resolution, *Gladiator* has as its ultimate horizon the renewal of Rome: the fall of the Empire is neither contemplated nor imagined. As Maximus says early in the film, when even Marcus Aurelius seems to question the achievements of Rome: "Rome is the light. I have seen the rest of the world. It is brutal and dark." Absent even the penumbra of Christianity – as one critic says, "Romans no longer need to turn into Christians to remain interesting to an American audience" – the film relies on the notion of a kind of mystic nationhood that will emerge from the relic Roman past, an image of nation that can be adapted to the contemporary context.[30]

As the film progresses, the increasingly spectacular scenes in the Colosseum take on a more explicit symbolic and political significance. Maximus, rather than being objectified and denied power through the scopic regime of the ring, gains authority through his performances. As Wyke has suggested, ancient Rome is reinvented here; the Colosseum itself is emptied of its traditional cinematic meaning and converted to the expression of a different message, a message that links punitive masculine agency with the rhetoric of social renewal and rebirth. In *Gladiator*, the "sand of the Colosseum," as one character says, not the "marble of the Senate," becomes the fertile setting for the regeneration of the Republic, and it is the body of the epic hero that releases this new life.

The Germs of New Life

In both *Spartacus* and *Gladiator*, the conflict resolves itself in a final confrontation in which the hero's grandeur and power are actualized. In both, there is an ultimate duel, a confrontation which is necessary to crystallize the hero's role as a representative of the collectivity. In *Spartacus*, however, the duel is not perfectly demarcated; its boundaries are difficult to define. Does it occur in the confrontation between Spartacus and Crassus, when Spartacus spits in Crassus' face, echoing Draba's blood spurting onto his face? Does it occur in the duel between Spartacus and his beloved Antoninus, each trying to kill the other out of mercy? Or is it rather the moment when the individual members of Spartacus' slave army declare their allegiance to the collectivity, each claiming to be Spartacus, each becoming capable of a heroic action equal to the situation?

In what is perhaps the most moving scene in the film, the captured army of Spartacus is pictured chained together and sitting on the dusty roadside, awaiting their fate. Crassus, the victorious general, announces that he will spare them the horrible fate of crucifixion if they will identify Spartacus to him. Spartacus is about to stand up and reveal himself when Antoninus, chained next to him, rises up and announces, "I am Spartacus." Immediately, several other soldiers stand up and claim to be Spartacus, repeating the line, "I'm Spartacus," until nearly the entire captured group has stood and proclaimed themselves to be him.

The scene described above has been interpreted as a direct reference to the infamous House Un-American Activities Commission, known popularly as the McCarthy Hearings, with its demand that witnesses "name names" of communist sympathizers. The novelist Howard Fast, who wrote the book on which the film is based, was jailed for his refusal to testify, and wrote the novel *Spartacus* while in prison. Dalton Trumbo, perhaps the most famous of the "Hollywood Ten," also refused to "name names" and was jailed and then blacklisted in Hollywood for many years.

In dramatizing the refusal of Spartacus' soldiers to "name names," the film brings the present-day context of the film's production into immediate focus.[31] But it also provides a moment of apotheosis, the moment when the male epic hero becomes an idealized figure, something more than human, not just a name, but a sign, a symbol of historical emergence. The collective identification of the former slaves with Spartacus translates the character into a transcendent figure, giving his name a symbolic potency that rivals that of Rome.

In *Gladiator*, a similar collective emergence is expressed through the solidarity of the gladiators. The composition of this corps of gladiators, who come from Germania, Africa, Spain, and Gaul, represents the margins of the Empire, the radial points. Where *Gladiator* departs from *Spartacus*, however, is in its use of the spectacle of martial combat to express the emergence of this new collectivity. This is expressed most directly in the scene of Maximus' duel with the famous "Tigris of Gaul," the only gladiator to have retired undefeated from the Roman arena. Perhaps the most sensationalized scene of combat in the entire film, the battle gives Maximus access to the equalizing power of spectacle, evoking the battle between Spartacus and Draba but transforming it to the expression of a different message. Here, with the game rigged against him, Maximus defeats the vaunted gladiator. Despite Commodus' insistent command of "thumbs down," Maximus appropriates the sovereign gesture by sparing the life of his abject opponent. He extends the sovereign gesture of sparing life (as Rodrigo in *El Cid* says, "anyone can take a life, but only a king can give life"), recalling to the Roman citizens in the Colosseum the basis of sovereignty, the power to grant an exception to bare life. The Roman audience immediately starts chanting, "Maximus the Merciful," a phrase that effectively shifts the sovereign power of exception from Commodus to Maximus, as if the gladiator-slave had here pushed through to take up the position of sovereignty. Like Draba, Maximus performs an act of self-authorship through martial combat and mercy, claiming the power of exception. Like Spartacus at the end of the film, Maximus becomes the focus of collective identification, an ideal, a symbol to rival that of Rome. Unlike Spartacus, however, the apotheosis of Maximus takes place in the arena, reclaiming a space identified with dehumanizing spectacle as a space of collective renewal.

Roland Barthes compares the experience of viewing the widescreen epic as akin to standing "on the balcony of History," and describes the stretched-out frontality of the epic screen as "the ideal space of the great dramaturgies."[32] In its closing scenes, *Gladiator* employs all the resources of epic spectacle in order to dramatize the replacing of a pathogenic

FIGURE 3.5 The only undefeated gladiator in the history of Rome, Tigris of Gaul, is defeated by Maximus (Russell Crowe). This sets up a scene that echoes *Spartacus*, as Maximus refuses to kill Tigris of Gaul, despite the "thumbs down" of Emperor Commodus (Joaquin Phoenix). *Gladiator* (2000) [DreamWorks SKG/Photofest]

historical structure with an exemplary one. Rome is depicted as an empire whose excesses and pathologies have been concentrated in the spectacles staged in the Colosseum. The spectacle of the Colosseum, however, is also depicted as the source of its renewal, the place from which it is issued a pardon. In the intensive focus on the action of the climactic duel between Commodus and Maximus, it is the spectacle itself that actualizes the possibility of regeneration. Spiraling down to this one moment of action, the film defines the space of the Colosseum, the action of the duel, and the gaze of the Roman spectators as the essence of an epoch, the concentrated and distilled point of Roman history. Spiraling out, it also suggests a new milieu, a new situation: the film uses the spectacle of the Colosseum to create an "originary world," to use Deleuze's expression, one that places the senators, the gladiators, the Praetorian Guard, the nobility, the slaves, and the citizens of Rome all on the same level platform, a world that departs from the historical setting of the ancient past and confers on Rome a different future.

After Maximus has been killed, Juba is viewed alone in the Colosseum. Here he buries Maximus' figurines of his family and ancestors in the dirt

FIGURE 3.6 Lucilla (Connie Nielsen) tells Maximus (Russell Crowe) he can "go to them," as he passes into Elysium. Maximus' death in the sand of the Colosseum provides the germs of new life. *Gladiator* (2000) [DreamWorks SKG/Photofest]

of the Colosseum floor. These small carved figurines had been treasured by Maximus, serving as tangible reminders of his family and as objects of veneration and prayer. Recalling Maximus' practice of rubbing dirt between his hands before a battle, Juba covers the figurines with the sand of the Colosseum, raises his head, and states: "Now we're free, and we'll see you again. But not yet. Not yet." The planting of the figurines by the black gladiator, with its clear suggestion of an appeal to the future, can be read as a symbol of the planting of the seeds of a new nation, a new civilization. As the camera rises up above the Colosseum to disclose the horizon of Rome and the mountains and sky beyond, illuminated by a setting sun, Rome becomes what Deleuze calls the "germinating stock" which prefigures America. The ancient past has brought into view the germs of new life. The analogical or parallel conception of history that underpins the epic is clearly evoked here, as the great moments of humanity communicate "via the peaks." With the return of the epic as a major genre in American cinema, *Gladiator* stands as a conspicuous example of a film that sets up a dialogue between the sedimented memories of history and nation preserved in genre form and alternative projects of national imagining.

Notes

1   For discussion of the concept of "genre memory," see Gary Saul Morson and Caryl Emerson, *Mikhail Bakhtin: Creation of a Prosaics* (Stanford, CA: Stanford University Press, 1990): 278–97.

2   Allan Barra quotes the British critic Paul Coates in "The Incredible Shrinking Epic," *American Film* 14(5) (March 1989): 40–5. See also Vivian Sobchack, "Surge and Splendor: A Phenomenology of the Historical Epic," *Representations* 29 (Winter 1990): 24–49.

3   See, for example, Monica Cyrino, *Big Screen Rome* (Malden, MA: Blackwell, 2005); Maria Wyke, *Projecting the Past: Ancient Rome, Cinema, and History* (London: Routledge, 1997); Bruce Babington and Peter William Evans, *Biblical Epics: Sacred Narrative in the Hollywood Cinema* (Manchester: Manchester University Press, 1993); Monica Cyrino, *Big Screen Rome* (Malden, MA: Blackwell, 2005); Martin Winkler, ed., *Gladiator: Film and History* (Malden, MA: Blackwell, 2004); Martin Winkler, ed., *Troy: From Homer's Iliad to Hollywood Epic* (Malden, MA: Blackwell, 2007).

4   Gilles Deleuze, *Cinema I: The Movement-Image* (Minneapolis: University of Minnesota Press, 1986): 148–51.

5   Michael Wood, *America in the Movies: Or, "Santa Maria, It Had Slipped My Mind"* (London: Secker & Warburg, 1975): 173.

6   Wyke, *Projecting the Past*: 33.
7   Arthur J. Pomeroy, "The Vision of a Fascist Rome in Gladiator," in Winkler, *Gladiator*: 111–23.
8   Deleuze, *Cinema I*, p. 149.
9   Ibid.: 146–7.
10 Leon Hunt, "What Are Big Boys Made Of? *Spartacus, El Cid*, and the Male Epic," in Pat Kirkham and Janet Thumin, *You Tarzan: Masculinity, Movies, and Men* (New York: St. Martin's Press, 1993): 81.
11 See Tara Godvin, "Tattoos become personal memorials to Sept. 11 and most loved ones" (www.Boston.com). See also Coco McPherson, "That Was Then, This Is Now," *Rolling Stone* 905 (September 19, 2002): 90–6.
12 Kim Hewitt, *Mutilating the Body* (Bowling Green, OH: Bowling Green State University Popular Press, 1997).
13 Ibid.
14 Paul Willeman, "Anthony Mann: Looking at the Male," *Framework* 15/16/17 (Summer 1981): 18.
15 Friedrich Nietzsche found a similar appeal in epic literature as well. Writing about the "will to power" displayed in the Greco-roman fascination with agonistic battle, he stresses "the visual stimulation of seeing muscular bodies in vigorous exertion, defying death and injury." See Ekhart Koehne, Cornelia Egwigleben, and Ralph Jackson, eds., *Gladiators and Caesars: The Power of Spectacle in Ancient Rome* (London: British Museum Press, 2000): 47.
16 Natalie Zemon Davis, "Trumbo and Kubrick Argue History," *Raritan* XXII:1 (Summer 1981): 173–90.
17 Maria Wyke, "*Spartacus:* Testing the Strength of the Body Politic," in *Projecting the Past*: 34–72.
18 See Rob Wilson, "Ridley Scott's *Gladiator* and the Spectacle of Empire: Global/Local Rumblings inside the Pax Americana," *European Journal of American Culture*, 21(2) (2002): 62–73. See also Brian J. White, "*American Beauty, Gladiator*, and the New Imperial Humanitarianism," *Global Media Journal* 1(1): 1–36.
19 Wilson, "Ridley Scott's *Gladiator*": 71.
20 See Mark Jancovich, "'The Purest Knight of All': Nation, History, and Representation in *El Cid*," *Cinema Journal* 40(1) (Fall 2000): 79–103.
21 In channeling messages of emergence and liberation through the spectacularized body, the epic film would seem to solicit a different critical understanding than that of static spectacle so often associated with the display of the female body in film.
22 The contemporary theorist Giorgio Agamben draws attention to the link between bare life and sovereignty in *Homo Sacer: Sovereign Power and Bare Life*, trans. Daniel Heller-Roazen (Stanford, CA: Stanford University Press, 1998).

23 Ina Rae Hark, "Animals or Romans: Looking at Masculinity in *Spartacus*," in Steven Cohan and Ina Rae Hark, eds., *Screening the Male: Exploring Masculinities in Hollywood Cinema* (London: Routledge, 1993): 151–72.

24 Woody Strode's antiracist identity was well established: he was the first black athlete to play in the National Football League, and was a teammate of Jackie Robinson at UCLA.

25 Keith Hopkins, *Conquerors and Slaves* (Cambridge: Cambridge University Press, 1978): 112. Quoted in Sandra R. Joshel and Sheila Murnaghan, "Introduction," *Women and Slaves in Greco-Roman Culture* (London: Routledge, 1998): 18.

26 M. I. Finley, "Was Greek Civilization Based on Slave Labor?," *Historia* 8 (1959): 145–64, reprinted in Finley, ed., *Slavery in Classical Antiquity: Views and Controversies* (New York: Barnes & Noble, 1968).

27 Nathan Huggins, "The Deforming Mirror of Truth: Slavery and the Master Narrative of American History," *Radical History Review* (Winter 1991): 37.

28 See Koehne et al., *Gladiators and Caesars*: 47.

29 Richard Slotkin, *Regeneration Through Violence* (Middletown, CT: Wesleyan University Press, 1973).

30 White, "*American Beauty, Gladiator*, and the New Imperial Humanitarianism": 24.

31 See especially Wyke, "*Spartacus*: Testing the Strength of the Body Politic," in *Projecting the Past*, and Cyrino, "*Spartacus*," in *Big Screen Rome*.

32 Roland Barthes, "On CinemaScope," trans. Jonathon Rosenbaum; see Jonathon Rosenbaum and James Morrison (http://social.chass.ncsu.edu/jiuvert/v313/barth.html) (first published in *Les letters nouvelles*, February 1954). James Morrison's illuminating analysis of Barthes's very short essay is particularly interesting.

CHAPTER 4

THE BIOGRAPHICAL FILM: *SCHINDLER'S LIST*

The release of *Schindler's List* in 1993 marked a turning point in representations of the Holocaust, altering the way the Holocaust is remembered and discussed. For the generation that had lived through World War II, Holocaust remembrance had been largely restricted to personal memories based on survivors' experiences. Although a number of feature films had referred to the Holocaust, many critics and theorists held that the Holocaust itself was essentially "unrepresentable," an event whose scale and horror could not be expressed in words or images, an event that ruptured history and defied any attempt to render it. In the words of one prominent filmmaker, the Holocaust erected a "ring of fire around itself, a borderline that cannot be crossed."[1] The global visibility and success of *Schindler's List*, however, highlighted the changing role of the mass media in Holocaust remembrance, and provoked a widespread debate about the importance of the media in preserving the lessons of the past for the present.

The critical anxiety about Holocaust representation prior to *Schindler's List* was especially emphatic when it came to fiction films. Several Holocaust authors, including Elie Weisel, offered the opinion that to make a film about the Holocaust was a violation: "One does not imagine the unimaginable, and in particular, one does not show it on screen."[2] In the contemporary period, however, the Holocaust has become a mainstream subject of film, television, and other cultural forms. The subject of a Pulitzer Prize-winning graphic novel, of community reenactments and theater performances in Israel, of two Academy Award-winning films, television series, and numerous museum and memorial projects throughout the world, the Holocaust is now considered one of the most important events in the history of modernity.[3] Among all these projects commemorating the Holocaust, *Schindler's List* has generally been acknowledged as the most consequential, the "jewel in the crown" of Holocaust representation, for more than any other work it desacralized the taboo on imagining the Holocaust in dramatic form and hurled it into mainstream consciousness. What had been regarded as a traumatic event that could not be represented in historical or fictional form is now considered a touchstone for national remembrance, for historical reconsideration, and for a new generation connecting to the past.

The critical reputation of the film, however, perhaps because of its influence and impact, has been mixed. Critics have assailed it for its portrayal of the Jews as passive and diminutive, its seeming fascination with female bodies, its three last-minute rescues, and its fictional inventions. Even more damaging to the film's critical reputation is its basic storyline – the focus on Oskar Schindler himself, a focus that renders the events of the Holocaust through the redemptive narrative of a German member of the Nazi Party, a hero whose conversion to the cause of rescuing Jews places the emphasis on an active, charismatic agent of history as opposed to the Jewish victims of the Nazi genocide. For many critics, the story of Schindler, a life shaped by historical events so morally repugnant that some feel they should not be represented at all, revises the Holocaust in a way that correlates too neatly with Hollywood values and aesthetics. Far from respecting the unique and absolute status of the Holocaust, *Schindler's List* seemed to transform the image of the Holocaust into a Hollywood narrative product, offering the illusion that the film medium can make sense of the trauma, contain it, and master it, a development that has turned the Holocaust into a form of "Shoah business."[4]

Nevertheless, *Schindler's List* offers a striking example of the cultural reach and power of mass media as a form of public memory, and the profound effects of mass culture on historical consciousness. The range of responses to the film in different countries is a striking example. In Germany, the film led to a wide-reaching public reassessment of ordinary German citizens' complicity in the genocide. For the first time, the Holocaust was openly acknowledged and debated in German society. Critics saw the film as an important, therapeutic event that broke German culture free of the amnesia and denial that had surrounded the subject of the genocide of the Jews. Perhaps understandably, the film also led to the sudden discovery of dozens of local Schindlers in German towns, previously unknown people who were found to have aided and rescued Jews during the Nazi period. In the United States critics saw the film as Steven Spielberg's rite of passage, a work that connected him to his Jewish heritage and marked his growth from child-centered narratives to adult subjects. The film was also understood as part of the "Americanization" of the Holocaust, a shift in focus from the Jews who perished to the Jews who survive in the New World, a reading augmented by the opening of the Holocaust Museum in Washington, DC the same year as the film was released, and by the passing of legislation in New Jersey mandating that the Holocaust and other genocides be taught in public schools. Critics in Israel, on the other hand, saw *Schindler's List* and the Holocaust Museum, in particular, as an appropriation of a key component of Jewish history. The film succeeded in redefining the discourse about the Holocaust in Israel. Until the 1990s, Israeli society did not embrace the victims of the Holocaust; the robust and militant identity that Israel promoted as its national self-image could not easily accommodate the victims of the genocide. Israeli society celebrated only the resistance fighters, those who actively fought against the Holocaust. Now, however, the central focus of the narrative has shifted to the survivors.[5]

But for all its success in provoking debates about memory, trauma, history, and national identity, one of the keys to understanding the affective reach and impact of the film has hardly been noticed – the extent to which *Schindler's List* draws on the forms and patterns of the biographical film. Illuminating the trauma of the historical past by focusing on an individual life, the film rehearses the generic patterns of the "biofilm," a form that has been an important and underappreciated part of the cinema's repertory of historical imagining. Although theorists have long decried the tendency to understand history in terms of the way an individual story reflects a collective historical event, Robert Rosenstone estimates that 80 percent of Hollywood historical films belong to the subgenre of the biographical film.[6] In recent years, the biographical film has seen an impressive return to popularity, with several serious and ambitious films on the lives of Howard Hughes, Ray Charles, Muhammad Ali, and Johnny Cash. Nevertheless, the biographical film has received very little critical attention, and even less critical appreciation.

Roland Barthes calls biography "the fiction that dare not speak its name," effectively capturing the sense of illegitimacy that seems to hover over projects that render history in terms of the trajectory of an individual life, an individual life which has been plotted and embellished according to the demands of storytelling.[7] In the case of the Holocaust, the sheer scale and magnitude of the event, the almost incomprehensible suffering of generations of Jews, and the deep and varied conflicts within German, Israeli, and American societies concerning the Holocaust would seem to argue against the validity of the biographical form as a means of representing this singular event.

The argument I will pursue here is that *Schindler's List* reinvents and repurposes the biographical film as a modernist form, communicating to a world audience in a popular, comprehensible idiom while at the same time utilizing advanced visual, acoustic, and narrative techniques. Hansen calls this popular style a form of "vernacular modernism," and argues that *Schindler's List* revives a kind of popular modernism that imbued films such as *Citizen Kane*, a quintessential modernist text that was also structured as an experimental biography.[8] Following Hansen, I argue that *Schindler's List* can be understood as an innovative project of historical representation, closer to *Citizen Kane* than to mainstream Hollywood cinema, one that uses a modernist vocabulary to refashion an established genre form.

In the words of one critic, the film's Schindler is a true Brechtian character. He is a con man and opportunist installed at the heart of a vastly more sinister criminal enterprise which ironically claims to be "legal."[9] A failure in his earlier business ventures, he succeeds in wresting good out of evil through bribery, flattery, and personal interest. Schindler becomes a savior of the Jews almost in spite of himself, a full-blown confidence man whose skills at corruption create an "absolute good." The historical milieu of the Nazi period allows a new kind of hero to emerge, a character defined by contradiction, whose vices are recoded – by way of the historical situation – as virtues.

One writer has said that *Schindler's List* is "composed of vertical scenes that develop the Schindler story and horizontal scenes that re-create the Holocaust in broader terms."[10] This is a useful but somewhat limited metaphor for picturing the dual orientation of the film. The vertical scenes of character development – the moments when Schindler's character is most fully revealed – are folded together with graphic and wrenching depictions of the persecution of the Jews. Using devices such as a moving camera and cross-cutting, Spielberg integrates the story of Schindler and the story of the Holocaust at the textual level by embedding Schindler in the heart of the larger story. Rather than proceeding along separate axes, the narrative and visual design of the film connects the story of Schindler with the story of the Holocaust from the perspective of both the victims and the perpetrators in a way that interlaces the biographical and the historical. Where the modernist masterpiece *Citizen Kane* suggests that narrative form, and especially the intricate structures of visual narration, obscures as much as it reveals about a person, *Schindler's List* suggests that narrative and visual form can illuminate the critical duality of character and history.

Collective Seduction

The opening sequence exemplifies the film's complexity of narrative address. Beginning with a scene of a Jewish family singing the Shabbat prayer over two lit candles, the film opens with an interior scene suffused with golden light. The prayer of thanks, the warm interior setting, and the familial cohesiveness pictured here create a reassuring sense of long custom and continuity. The scene is nonspecific in terms of place and time, but the setting appears to be an apartment in Europe in the 1930s or 1940s. A series of dissolves brings us to a close-up of the candles, and the words *Schindler's List* appear precisely in the middle, between them. Focusing on one candle as it extinguishes itself, we see a thin line of smoke drifting toward the ceiling. As the camera follows the smoke, a match cut occurs: the film jumps to an exterior shot in black and white of a dense plume of smoke accompanied by the loud, high-pitched screech of a train whistle. The camera begins tilting downwards, reversing its earlier direction, as we follow the train into a station.

The opening moments of the film function as an overture, offering an abbreviated and highly symbolic representation of the themes of the film. To begin with, the Shabbat ceremony serves as a call to commemoration, to keep holy the Sabbath, evoking the theme of remembrance as well as the protection of the covenant, the biblical promise of the preservation of the Jewish people. The increasingly close shots of the candles provide a condensed visualization of the passing of time. When the candle burns out, the message communicated by the smoke suggests and recalls the original meaning of the word holocaust: a burnt offering, a sacrifice made with fire. The opening sequence embeds these images and messages in a way that echoes the larger structures of the film, as well as introducing several motifs that will recur throughout. Here, the film underlines its own role as an act of commemoration.

As the train pulls into the station, the camera details one or two men in suits and overcoats setting up portable tables and typewriters on the sidewalk. The few tables become a vast row, as the names of Jews coming into Kraków are recorded, haltingly, but painstakingly. The scene alternates shots of the pages being typed with full-face portrait shots of the Jews coming into the city. Their faces are open, their manner friendly; their style of dress suggests that they come from the rural districts. This is immediately contrasted with our first images of Schindler. Far from beginning with a name and a face, Schindler is introduced in a series of stylized close-ups of hands attaching cufflinks, selecting a tie, pouring a whiskey, distributing large wads of money to his various pockets. Finally, he attaches a Nazi Party pin to his lapel. A long, graceful camera movement tracks Schindler's entrance into the nightclub where he will conduct his business. A tango is heard from the band performing on stage. Only after Schindler has been seated in a prime central location does the camera circle around from the back to reveal his face, whose handsomeness is underlined by the admiring and inviting gaze of a female patron shown immediately afterward, and emphasized by the lighting cameraman's technique of directing a beam of light into the actor Liam Neeson's eyes, giving them a perpetual twinkle.

The contrast with the opening portrait shots of the Jews is stark. The film cuts from a grainy, flat documentary style of lighting to glamorous 1930s-style studio lighting; it shifts from a series of homely, ethnic-looking people rendered in unflattering extreme close-up to a drifting, languorous camera movement that highlights and reinforces the sensuality of the main character; it moves from the sound of a train whistle and the erratic percussion of a series of typewriters to a seductive tango that works in tandem with the choreography of the character's entrance into the nightclub. As Schindler begins plying his charm and making friendly overtures to the Nazi officers who frequent the club, the question is repeatedly asked, "Who is that man?" As the evening progresses, Schindler turns the nightclub into a private party, with Nazi officers, their girlfriends, the cabaret showgirls, and the maitre-d' all vying for his attention. Finally, after a long evening of festivities, the maitre-d' answers another inquiry with an almost giddy, "That's Oskar Schindler!"

Reminiscent of the banquet scene in *Citizen Kane*, the introduction of Schindler climaxes with a series of flash photographs, as first one group of Nazis and then another poses with Schindler and the showgirls. The scene unfolds as a collective seduction, as first the women, then the Nazi

FIGURE 4.1 The glamorous Oskar Schindler (Liam Neeson), ready for his close-up – the climax of an elaborate cinematic introduction detailing all the accoutrements of Schindler's "presentation." Schindler's List (1993) [Universal Pictures/Photofest]

officers, the waiters, and the restaurant staff are captivated by his charm and lavish spending. At the beginning of the banquet scene in *Citizen Kane*, the main character looks at the group of renowned reporters he has assembled and states that earlier, when looking at an identical photograph in the window of the rival newspaper, the *Chronicle*, he felt like a kid outside a candy store. Now, however, "I've gotten all my candy." A similar mood is set in the opening here; the glossy photography, the available women, the feasting, create a sense of indulgence and excess. Most striking of all is the ease with which Schindler manages this. The world of Nazi Kraków has opened itself to him like an oyster.

The first section of the film is divided between the increasing persecution of the Jews in Kraków and the growing business influence and success of Schindler. With money supplied secretly by Jewish investors, Schindler buys an abandoned metalware factory and begins making field cookware for the Nazi troops. The keeping of the books, which must be double-entered to conceal the bribes paid to requisitions officers, is conducted by Stern, a Jewish accountant who also assembles the workforce from the Jewish community in Kraków. Early scenes between Stern and Schindler are played for comic contrast: Schindler is urbane, strikingly

FIGURE 4.2 Oskar Schindler (Liam Neeson) as Charlie Kane, surrounded by his new best friends. Schindler's success in attracting the Nazi power brokers of Kraków unfolds in a dazzling montage that recalls the banquet scene of *Citizen Kane*. *Schindler's List* (1993) [Universal Pictures/Photofest]

confident, and devoted only to himself. Stern is self-effacing, seemingly without personal ambition or desire, and committed to helping the most helpless among his many Jewish friends and acquaintances, including a musician, a professor of history, and a one-armed, elderly man. The Jewish men are portrayed, for the most part, as small, childlike, and unattractive. The Jewish women are attractive, active, and aware, depictions that have been much noted by critics of the film. On the whole, the film in its first third plays out as a somewhat dark version of a ghetto comedy, full of amusing stereotypes, with a likeable cad as a protagonist.

The issues of character, stereotype, and perspective that dominate criticism of the film are usually centered on the relationship of Schindler to Yitzhak Stern, on the one hand, and Amon Goeth, the camp commandant at Plaszow, on the other. Stern, according to this line of criticism, pulls Schindler in a positive, compassionate direction, calmly informing him of the brutality of the Nazis, quietly advocating for certain people to be added to the workforce, raising Schindler's consciousness in subtle and incremental ways. Goeth, on the other hand, befriends Schindler, extends him special considerations, and draws explicit comparisons between them. Both relationships have been described by some critics as homoerotic: Stern, as one critic says, is feminized in relation to Schindler, playing a version of the quiet "good woman" behind every successful man, facilitating Schindler's career by working behind the scenes to take care of production schedules, bribes, and payoffs. Theirs is a "marriage" of convenience, the critic argues, but eventually, they grow to appreciate and love one another, and consummate their union by sharing a drink together – a gesture Stern had several times earlier refused.[11] The relationship between Goeth and Schindler, on the other hand, is one of seeming mutual admiration. Goeth is attracted to Schindler's wardrobe and style, and admires his success with women. For his part, Schindler appreciates the favors Goeth extends him, making the point that if it weren't for the war, Goeth would be a decent fellow, a point that Stern quickly and decisively refutes. Schindler and Goeth are linked in a series of visual parallels, set up so as to illustrate what one writer calls "styles of masculinity." In one cross-cut sequence, we see both men shaving in front of a mirror, an activity that Stern is never portrayed performing. Where Schindler and Stern are presented as contrasts, Schindler and Goeth are presented as variants of masculinity. Geoffrey Hartman writes that "both Schindler and Goeth remain stylized figures that fail to transcend the handsome silhouettes of the average Hollywood film."[12]

The admiring homosociality that suffuses almost every scene involving Schindler and the Nazis underscores the ambiguity of Schindler's conversion to rescuer of the Jews. Many critics have commented on the fact that Schindler's motivations for altruism seem murky throughout, and his moment of conversion is never visualized or highlighted. This violates one of the cardinal tenets of the classic biographical film, laid out most explicitly by Darryl Zanuck, the studio executive who developed the biopic as a major genre form. Zanuck insisted on a clearly established "rooting interest" for the audience. As George Custen summarizes, "a Zanuck famous person had to have clear motivation for the decisions that brought him or her greatness. Actions had to be communicated to the audience in a telegraphic scene or two which served as an explanation of the forces that drove the person to achieve his or her unusual destiny."[13] Zanuck instructed his writers to provide explanations for the hero's achievements, insisting on explicit motivation and clear-cut rooting interest. Zanuck also offset the unique achievements of the hero with the domestic familiarity of an ordinary family life or a love interest. By contrast, the formative experiences that supposedly shape a character are never visualized in *Schindler's List*: his altruism is never connected to past experience or to a manifest change in consciousness. Far from securing the audience's "rooting interest" by depicting an ordinary and fulfilling domestic life, Spielberg depicts Schindler as chronically subject to carnal temptation; his wife is a minimal presence in the narrative, he has at least two girlfriends in Kraków, and appears to have easy access to any number of others. Rather than being driven by internal energies and convictions that make him stand out from the world, Schindler seems to be utterly defined and shaped by the social and historical world that he inhabits.

With explicit motivation missing and rooting interest denied, Schindler nevertheless occupies the center of the story. The important and perennial questions that circulate around the Holocaust are conveyed in a way that is defamiliarized by the focus on Schindler, given a unique twist. Issues such as the extent and limits of human empathy, the chance decisions that mean life or death, the guilt of the survivor, and the psychology of evil become interwoven with the discovery of Schindler's character, the growth of his moral character. This is conveyed by interweaving the Jewish story of the Holocaust and survival with Schindler's growing consciousness of the extended human response that he is called upon to offer. And here the lack of family and the absence of a "rooting interest" in the portrayal of Schindler serve a strategic interest: the "Schindler Jews," as they come to be called, serve the role occupied by the family and domesticity in the classical biopic. Schindler's lack of a family and the absence of his wife create a symbolic space that is filled by the Jewish workers.

Spielberg prepares the viewer for the interweaving of the Jewish story with Schindler's consciousness in a scene that is symbolically pivotal. Schindler is ensconced in his office above the enamelware factory, just beginning to eat his lunch. His large office windows look out on the factory floor, where we see a factory flame burning in the background. The business is proving to be successful for all concerned: Schindler extends protection to the Jewish workers, who are deemed to be "essential workers"; they in turn provide free labor, which translates into enormous profits for Schindler. An air of complacent self-satisfaction permeates Schindler's personal bearing. Stern informs him that one of the workers would like to speak to him, to thank him, and that this worker has been coming every day. Schindler reluctantly agrees to see the man, and Stern opens the door to a small, white-haired, older man with one arm. The old man, who appears to be half Schindler's height, gratefully tells him that he wishes to thank him for his job, for protecting a one-armed man as an "essential worker." As Schindler accepts the man's thanks, and makes to hurry him along, the old man seems to want to continue. He insists on saying to Schindler, with absolute conviction: "You are a good man. You are a good man." Schindler accepts the compliment and ushers him to the door. Now the camera changes position, cutting from an eye-level two-shot of the conversation to a low-angle shot set at the height of the table with Schindler's lunch. Another plate is positioned on the table, as if for a guest. Schindler, perturbed, closes the door and walks back to his position near the table. The scene cuts to the outside of the factory, as Schindler walks out briskly with Stern and strongly warns him, "Don't ever let that happen again!"

The innocuousness of the scene disguises its critical function. More than simply foreshadowing the transformation of Schindler, who eventually will become utterly committed to the saving of his Jewish workers, the scene illustrates the complex layering of messages concerning character provided by the filmic discourse. Schindler seems entirely unworthy of the praise offered by the old man, as the profits provided by the free labor of the Jews at this point seem to be his sole motivation. Moreover, his behavior toward the old man is initially condescending, and finally brusque. But the film-text, the details of the *mise en scène* and camera placement suggest something more. With the tongue of flame in the background, the unmotivated cut to the invisible guest at the table, and the empty plate waiting to be taken up, Schindler is inscribed in a pictorial frame full of Jewish symbolism. The old man's judgment of Schindler serves as a kind of benediction, creating a thematic bridge to the scenes that will follow.

Immediately afterward, the Schindler Jews are intercepted on their way to the factory by a Nazi patrol. Mocking the protests of the Jews that they are "essential workers," the Nazis roughly order the Jews to begin shoveling snow. As they notice the one-armed old man having trouble with the shovel, they take him aside and shoot him in the head. As he is seen lying face-up, the blood pours out and streams onto the white snow. Although Schindler is not present at the scene, the sequencing and timing of the shots, along with the use of voiceover, places him at the center of the scene's narration. The sequence begins with a voiceover – "You shouldn't think of them as yours, Oskar . . . – placed over shots of the workers beginning to shovel snow. The camera cross-cuts to the German officer's chambers; he and Schindler are drinking a glass of schnapps. The film then cuts to a medium shot of the one-armed man shoveling snow, amid a group of Schindler's workers. German soldiers notice the man and lead him away, saying, "A one-armed Jew. Twice as useless!" The camera now cross-cuts back to the German office. We realize that the snow-shoveling scene took place the day before, and that Schindler has come to the German's office to register a complaint. He points out, strongly: "I lost a day of production." Another cross-cut brings us back to the snow scene, which continues with a low-angle shot showing Stern with a worried look on his face, and then to another low-angle shot of one of the Schindler Jews, Mrs. Rosner, and her little bespectacled girl, Danka, who is watching the old man being taken away. Her mother commands her to look away, to "Look at the snow! Look at the snow!" The camera is then repositioned between the rows of snow shovelers, with the old man in long shot at the end of what looks like a tunnel of arms wielding shovels. A German soldier puts a pistol to the back of his head and shoots him. He falls to the ground, as the snow continues to be shoveled, thrown across the camera's view. The camera cuts again to Schindler: "I lost a worker. I expect to be compensated." Another cross-cut follows to a close-up of the old man, eyes looking into the camera, blood flowing from his head. The camera follows the stream of blood. As the German's voice is heard on the soundtrack, we cut back to the office: "The Chancellor said that to believe Jewish workers have a vital place in Reich economics is a treasonable offense. A one-armed machinist? Really, Oskar." For the first time, the camera cuts to a full-face portrait shot of Schindler, as he says: "He was a metal press operator," followed by an even closer shot as he states emphatically: "Quite skilled."

The filmic discourse here provides a layered portrayal of character and event. Schindler's protest concerning lost productivity, the seemingly cold actuarial quality of the discourse, frame the scene in a way that defamiliarizes it. Muting its melodramatic potential, the dialogue about productivity and compensation serves as a distancing device that doubles the impact of the final close-up shots. Although most of the scene portrays Schindler in medium shot, in shadow and in profile, his Nazi lapel-pin gleaming, the last shots in the sequence deliver an emotional exclamation point. Seen in close-up and full face immediately following the close-up of the old man dead in the snow, Schindler's anger is revealed with perfect clarity. In the final two shots of the sequence, Schindler's essential character seems to be revealed; he appears to be motivated by the righteous outrage that recalls his designation as a "good man" in the preceding scene.

Spielberg's complex style of cinematic narration is strikingly effective in integrating what has been called the "vertical" and the "horizontal" axes of the story – the development of character and the unfolding of the Holocaust narrative. The use of *mise en scène* and camera placement in the scene in which the old man expresses his gratitude, and the use of cross-cutting and voice-over in the snow shoveling scene express the incorporation of Schindler into the Jewish story as well as a certain sense of resistance on Schindler's part. In the sequence that immediately follows the snow-shoveling scene, Spielberg opens the curtain on the Holocaust a little wider, suggesting something of the scale of the persecution of the Jews. Schindler has arrived at the train station just in time to save Stern from being shipped off to Auschwitz. As they walk side by side along the platform, Stern remonstrates with himself for leaving his "essential worker" pass at home, for being "stupid." Schindler interrupts him by asking demeaningly, "What would have happened if I had been five minutes later! Where would I be then?" Stern, who had been walking abreast of Schindler, bows his head and essentially fades into the background, humiliated by Schindler's cold attitude. As they depart the platform, however, Stern casts his glance at a baggage cart filled with suitcases and steamer trunks – the property of the Jews on the train, luggage that will never arrive. The camera now focuses on the cart as it is wheeled into a station warehouse, and follows the transit of the baggage. The warehouse has been turned into a sorting station: huge piles of shoes, smaller piles of jewelry, and enormous collections of photographs. One man with an eyepiece has the job of removing the jewels from watches. In the last shot of the scene, he is given a large collection of gold-filled teeth to deal with.

In this scene, Spielberg uses the camera and the *mise en scène* to comment on the scale of the destruction, and to contrast Schindler's self-absorption with the horror of the genocide now taking place. The message we take from the sequence extends well beyond the perspectives of Schindler and Stern: Spielberg uses the camera as an independent instrument of commentary and description, rendering the facts of the historical world in concrete detail and articulating the magnitude of the Holocaust in a way that exceeds the frame of knowledge of the protagonists. The technique can be compared to D. W. Griffith's innovative use of the iris shot in *The Birth of a Nation*. Here, a mother and her children are shown in a small-aperture iris shot huddled on a hillside, watching a few soldiers below. The aperture of the lens then widens, to reveal an entire panorama of battling armies, an effect that dilates the historical frame from the perspective of one character to suggest the enormous scale of the historical event. Spielberg creates a similar effect at various points in the film through camera movement, cross-cutting, and ellipses, establishing several new devices for historical narration in the process.

"Today is History"

One of the most distinctive narrative strategies employed in the film is the splitting of narrative focus between Schindler and Goeth, the commandant of the forced labor camp at Plaszow. Directly after Goeth is introduced, the film presents a series of close-ups of each man shaving, shots that seem to emphasize the dualism of the two characters. Goeth then delivers a speech to the assembled German officers and soldiers, preparing them, in terms that recall the famous speech by Himmler, for the liquidation of the ghetto, which they are about to put into action. "Today is history." Goeth narrates the story of the culture the Nazis are about to destroy; he tells us that the Jews came from Russia 600 years ago, "with nothing. Nothing." He talks about how they flourished and prospered, and lived successfully in Kraków for hundreds of years. Tomorrow, he says, this culture will be a rumor, it didn't exist. Your children will wonder about this day, he tells the German soldiers. "Today is history."

As Goeth is speaking, the cinematic narration illustrates his words with a series of representative scenes of the Schindler Jews in the ghetto going about their daily business, including a scene of a rabbi praying, a family at table with the father slicing bread, and a man and a woman looking at each other with tangible, heartfelt love in their eyes. As the familial, pleasing images of the Jews are seen, Goeth's speech continues to be heard. The sound of the rabbi praying is also audible on the soundtrack. Finally, we have a shot of Stern drinking tea, buttoning his vest, and looking out his window to see rows of tables and chairs being set up to record the names of those about to be taken from the ghetto. The scene ends with a shot of Schindler riding in a field with his girlfriend, and coming to a halt on a promontory overlooking the city.

The complex narrative design of this scene illuminates the broad outlines of the historical argument Spielberg sets forth. Beginning with a speech grounded in historical fact – Goeth's speech is a close echo of Himmler's Poznan speech to the SS – Spielberg overlays specific concrete details of the Jewish culture about to be liquidated.[14] The warm, homely quality of these scenes of life in the Kraków ghetto conveys a sharp poignancy: with Goeth's speech echoing on the soundtrack, we feel we are looking at a world that is already lost, at moving snapshots of a life that will imminently pass into oblivion. However, a competing message emerges here as well. Goeth speaks in portentous tones that echo on the soundtrack, suggesting a vast, unalterable process: "Today is history. Today will be remembered. The young will ask with wonder about this day. 600 years ago, Catherine the Great, so called, told the Jews they could live in Poland. They came here with nothing. Nothing. And they flourished . . . By this evening, those six centuries are a rumor. They never happened. Today is history." Yet Spielberg's images are equally potent in depicting ordinary life: prayer, the sharing of bread, the expression of marital love. These are the forces that will stand against the destructiveness of Nazi Germany and its plans for a thousand-year Reich. Moreover, as Goeth is heard on the soundtrack, the voice of the rabbi sings underneath, counterpointing Goeth's words with a message of continuity, of a deep cultural tradition that has outlasted empires and civilizations, that has persevered over millennia.

In this sequence Spielberg creates a subtle and effective historical argument by bifurcating the narrative voice. Splitting the narrative focus between Goeth and the Jews in the ghetto, the sequence simultaneously captures the historical reality of the liquidation of the ghetto, as well as suggesting the historical survival of the Jewish people. These two perspectives are interwoven throughout the film. The malign character of the Nazis is expressed in Goeth's pathological, unpredictable behavior, just as the quiet perseverance of the Jews is personalized in Stern.

The point where these two perspectives are joined is in the person of Schindler. The liquidation of the ghetto sequence is focalized through shots of Schindler riding in a field overlooking the ghetto with his girlfriend. As their horses sweep by the camera, Spielberg cuts to a matching shot of the wheels of Goeth's car moving past the camera into the ghetto. Schindler is then pictured watching the destruction of the Kraków ghetto from above the city while astride his horse. Many critics have said that this scene constitutes the turning point for Schindler, the point at which his sympathy for the Jews becomes fully manifest. Underlining this reading is the emphasis on the subjectivity of Schindler, as he spots a little girl and watches her traversing the city, seemingly oblivious to the carnage all around her, her red coat the one spot of color in the entire film apart from the Shabbat candle sequence at the beginning of the film and another candle sequence at the end.

The scene of the *Aktion* intricately weaves together what one critic has called the horizontal story of the Jews and the vertical development of Schindler's character. Lasting more than twenty minutes, the liquidation is rendered in a kind of staccato frenzy, a bedlam of noise and slaughter punctuated by acts of mercy as well as brutality. Filmed in a "verité" style with handheld cameras, the frenetic scenes of evacuation and killing are accompanied by a continuous cacophony of barking dogs, shouting, and the panic-inducing sounds of blaring loudspeakers, sirens, and machine-gun fire. Its realism led one survivor of the liquidation, one of the Schindler Jews, to say that the scenes "were so accurate that a participant like myself would not know that actual footage was not being used." Although the scene pummels the viewer with close-range barbarity, several intimate moments of human connection stand out: the doctor and nurse tenderly delivering poison to a ward of very ill patients so that they would not suffer from the Nazis; the kiss between Pfefferberg and his wife who "can't go in the sewers," a kiss whose timing saves Pfefferberg when the group immediately ahead of him is discovered in the sewers and machine-gunned; the last-second rescue of a mother and daughter, the Rosners, by a young Jewish boy working for the Nazis in exchange for his survival. These scenes of quiet, intimate drama are counterpointed by the frenzied barbarity of the Nazis, and by grim ironies: the Nazis using stethoscopes to detect the faint sounds of Jews hiding in secret closets and under trapdoors; the soldier playing classical piano as the carnage unfolds; the rampaging German who kills an older man in front of his family and then tries to elicit a smile from an infant. The combination of intimate moments and grotesque inversions of everyday life creates a surreal effect, a Guernica-like combination of macabre imagery and homely detail.

Schindler witnesses these events at a distance; the occasional cutbacks to his perspective are juxtaposed in a telling way to events in the ghetto. The first occurs just after the young boy, Adam, saves the Rosners, the mother and daughter who have been especially visible in scenes featuring the Schindler Jews. Walking with Adam so that he can "put them in the good line," the mother says to him, "you know our saying? . . . You are no longer a boy. I am saying a blessing for you." As she utters these words, the camera focuses in close-up on the boy's countenance, and dwells on his sober, haunting expression as a deep shadow falls on his face. At this point the camera cuts to Schindler, isolated in the frame. The juxtaposition of Adam and Schindler triggers several associations. Schindler, like Adam, is working for the Nazis; Schindler, like Adam, will "save a life." But their two trajectories through history appear, at this point in the narrative, to be starkly different. Schindler's focus now turns to the little girl in red, wandering through the ghetto. As the little girl appears in the scene, a children's song is heard on the soundtrack. As she traverses the ghetto, the sound of children's voices accompanies her. Schindler is shown watching her move from one macabre scene to another, moving through the streets as if sleepwalking, drifting by random killings, executions, and violent destruction, all of which she sees, a perspective that magnifies the dread.

The mystery of Schindler's character, which forms the hermeneutic outline of Thomas Keneally's biography, is only partially resolved in the *Aktion* scene, with its intermittent focus on Schindler's act of witnessing.[15] Where the classical and even the modern biographical film such as *Nixon*, *The Aviator*, *Walk the Line*, or *Ray*, insists on defining the causative process that catalyzes the development of character – typically dramatizing a traumatic or defining childhood experience and reiterating this moment at the "turning point" of the character's biography – *Schindler's List* keeps the biographical character at arm's length. Nor does the film appeal to discourses outside the frame of the film. In his well-regarded study of Hollywood biopics, George Custen emphasizes the link between the star persona of the actor and the character he or she is portraying. The star and character taken together form a dual object of admiration: we admire the character being portrayed, and "worship" the star portraying him or her.[16] Schindler, however, is played by Liam Neeson, who was relatively unknown at the time of the film's production, and who was chosen by Spielberg partly because of his anonymity. The mystery of Schindler is, in effect, compounded by the anonymity of the film's star, whose personality and character could not be inferred from discourses outside the frame.

Diabolical and Sainted Lives

In a well-known essay on biography, the Frankfurt School theorist Leo Lowenthal argued that biographies play a role in contemporary society similar to the role the "Lives of the Saints" played for earlier cultures, producing model lives that could be emulated by readers. Lowenthal discerned a certain degeneration in the subjects of magazine biographies in American culture over the first half of the twentieth century, however, finding that the most popular subjects of biographies had shifted from "models of production," such as Henry Ford and Thomas Edison, to "models of consumption," such as movie stars and other popular entertainers. This shift in focus coincided, in Lowenthal's view, with the rise of "mass culture" and the "culture industry," with its cults of celebrity and fame.[17] As Custen writes, "power through the making of the world had been replaced by power through ownership of its coveted items." The new forms of power afforded by the mass media could be attained by the "appropriation of a proper and glamorous appearance."[18] The opening half of *Schindler's List* seems to illustrate elements of Lowenthal's argument. Schindler attains his influence, his stature, precisely through the cultivation of a glamorous and successful image. He seems to inhabit a role derived from the more sophisticated films of the period, as if he were a character from the films of Ernst Lubitsch or Howard Hawks. One could imagine the character of Schindler in an American film of the 1930s, perhaps as a character who rises to social prominence through charm and guile and whose true, positive nature is revealed only at the end. With the clothing, mannerisms, and accoutrements of a modern cosmopolitan, Schindler constructs an image, a public persona that becomes a significant source of power. As he says to Stern early on in the film, he is no good at doing the work, it's "the presentation" at which he excels.

But it is the link Lowenthal makes between modern biography and the "Lives of the Saints" that is most intriguing for the purpose of understanding the genealogical imprint of the genre on *Schindler's List*. Just as Catholic hagiography depends upon the overt presence of evil in order to shape the life of the saint, so *Schindler's List* depends upon the pathology of Goeth and the persecution of the Jews to mold the character of Schindler. Goeth and Schindler are paired throughout the

FIGURE 4.3 Oskar Schindler (Liam Neeson) and Amon Goeth (Ralph Fiennes) discuss the fate of Helen Hirsch, Goeth's housekeeper. Goeth and Schindler are studies in contrasting "styles" of masculinity, a duality that excludes the central role played by Itzhak Stern (Ben Kingsley) in Schindler's journey. *Schindler's List* (1993) [Universal Pictures/Photofest]

middle portion of the film; for every malevolent act committed by Goeth, Schindler responds with an act of mercy. Schindler emerges as a subject worthy of emulation and admiration only through his proximity to absolute evil, as embodied in the character of Goeth.

The deepening sense of humanity that Schindler manifests as the film progresses is counterpointed to the sustained profile of sadism that defines Goeth. Visiting the work camp in order to cull workers to make room for new arrivals, Goeth decides an older man making hinges is not productive enough. He removes him to the entryway, has him kneel, and proceeds to try to execute him. After both his pistol and the pistol of his henchman repeatedly jam, he brutally beats the man on the head. Stern tells Schindler about this, who responds by quietly passing Stern his platinum lighter to bribe the Jewish clerk, Goldman, into placing the man in Schindler's factory. Following this scene, we next see Goeth in front of a line of Jews. Someone has stolen a chicken. Goeth shoots one man, and demands to know the culprit. After a desperately tense moment, the young boy Adam, who had earlier saved the Rosners by "putting them in the good line," steps forward. Yes, he tells Goeth, he knows who stole the chicken. As Goeth looks on, expecting that his brutal tactics will result in the betrayal of one Jew by another, Adam points to the dead man on the ground, "It was him!" Hearing the story from Stern, Schindler immediately gives Stern his cigarette case to facilitate the transfer of Adam. Next, Schindler is visited by a young woman who requests that her parents be placed under Schindler's protection. "Your factory is a haven," she tells Schindler. He flies into a rage, knowing how dangerous such a reputation can be, and remonstrates with Stern about spreading stories of Schindler's benevolence. "Goeth has a lot of pressure," he tells Stern. "War brings out the worst, always the worst. Without the war, he would be all right." Stern then tells him about a work detail from which a man had escaped. Goeth had lined them up and methodically shot every other man, twenty-five in all. Schindler changes his mind and arranges for the young woman's parents to work in his factory. Finally, Schindler visits the young Jewish woman Helen Hirsch, Goeth's housemaid and object of forbidden desire. Schindler asks her, "Do you know who I am? I am Schindler!" This scene has been interpreted as evidence of vainglory on Schindler's part, a revealing moment of narcissism, as if he had begun to believe his own legend. Helen responds by telling Schindler about her plight under Goeth, the fact that there are no rules you can follow. He kills people without cause or provocation. Schindler ends the conversation by assuring her that she is special and particular in Goeth's mind, and that he "enjoys

FIGURE 4.4 Amon Goeth (Ralph Fiennes) "selects" Helen Hirsch (Embeth Davidtz) to be his housekeeper. Her beauty makes her particularly vulnerable to Goeth, who imagines her as a forbidden temptress as well as his secret bride. *Schindler's List* (1993) [Universal Pictures/Photofest]

you too much" to kill her. Giving her a kiss on the forehead, he seals the promise, saying "Don't worry. It's not that kind of kiss."

What appears to be a contrastive portrait of the two men becomes a dual portrait, the comic and tragic versions of a single person during the scene of Schindler's birthday celebration. The sequence begins with a wedding being performed in the camp by an older Jewish woman. The young couple being married stand beneath a chuppah and the ceremony begins according to custom. The camera cuts to Goeth in his villa, filling his glass with brandy, and then to Schindler in what appears to be a nightclub, celebrating and being serenaded by a beautiful singer. The diegetic sound from each of the scenes carries over to the next, so that the sound of the blessing from the wedding ceremony is linked to the shots of Goeth, as well as to Schindler in the club. Following the shot of Schindler, the focus of the singer's ardent attentions, the film cuts to Goeth walking down to the cellar to speak with Helen. He speaks softly and seductively, complimenting her on her service as his maid, talking about loneliness, saying he would like to reach out and "touch you in your loneliness." Oddly, Goeth supplies both his half and Helen's half of an imagined dialogue as she stands stock still, silent and fearful, in a clinging white slip, seemingly soaking wet after what looks like an interrupted shower. The asynchronous sound of the nightclub singer is audible in the cellar, just as the sound of the Jewish wedding was audible in the earlier shots of Goeth. He approaches Helen, and begins touching her hair. "They compare you to insects, to vermin. I ask you, is this the face of a rat? Are these the eyes of a rat? Hath not a Jew eyes?" His hand gestures as he strokes her hair are rhymed with the next shot, focusing on the hand gestures of the singer seductively addressing her song to Schindler. As the film cuts back to Goeth, he says, "I feel for you, Helen." He begins to move his lips toward hers, at which point the camera cuts back to the Jewish wedding and to the violent explosion of a lightbulb being crushed underfoot, a stand-in for the glass that is traditionally crushed at the conclusion of a Jewish wedding. Goeth then tells Helen, "No. I don't think so. You nearly did it, didn't you?" Goeth then begins smashing Helen in the face, violently beating her, throwing her on the bed and pummeling her face. The applause from the wedding is carried over as Goeth beats her, merging with the sound of the applause from the nightclub. A fast series of cross-cuts ensues between the newly married couple kissing, Schindler kissing numerous women at the nightclub, and Goeth beating Helen, finally overturning a shelf on her. The scene then focuses only on Schindler, now at Goeth's villa, and on a pair of Jewish girls from the camp presenting him with a birthday cake. Schindler expresses his gratitude, and kisses the youngest one in a paternal way. He then kisses the older girl on the lips. Her near-panic at this violation of Nazi law is evident, and the alarmed looks of all around him testify to the potential consequences of this indiscretion.

The sensuality that suffuses the scene is offset by the threat of violence that pervades it. Helen, in a white slip, standing shivering in the cellar, is a victim standing symbolically as a bride. One pair of writers has compared this scene to the iconography of a horror film, emphasizing the wet hair of Helen, the clinging white slip, and the expressionistic lighting that casts the whole exchange in deep, sinister shadow. The beating of Helen, in this reading, is closely similar to the shower scene in *Psycho*, with its melding of violence and sexuality.[19] Modeled on the principle of intellectual montage, the construction of the scene brings Schindler and Goeth into a shared circuit of desire, with Helen, the forbidden Jewess, at the center. Here, Schindler's wild, promiscuous sexuality seems to inevitably drift to a young Jewish girl, a prisoner of the camps, a counterpart to Helen, the focus of Goeth's sadistic sexual desire and his imaginary bride. The Jewish wedding that initiates the scene overarches it with a symbolic meaning.

The film technique Spielberg employs here is used to create a series of parallels and contrasts. Perhaps the most well-known example in contemporary film of intellectual montage is the baptism sequence in *The Godfather*, in which Michael Corleone participates in the baptism of his son, Michael, while the camera reveals the simultaneous bloody murders of all of his rivals for power. The literal baptism is complemented by a symbolic baptism of Michael as Godfather. Another well-known example is the killing of Colonel Kurtz in *Apocalypse Now*. As Willard hacks Kurtz to death in the jungle compound, the camera cuts between the killing and the simultaneous slaughter of a sacred ox by Montagnard tribesmen. In *Schindler's List*, the three scenes of the wedding, the beating, and the birthday are rendered through cross-cutting in an accelerated tempo, coloring and infecting one another. Images of savagery are joined to images of pleasure and celebration to create a complex message. Although it is tempting to "read" these messages literally, it is at the level of suggestion that these sequences are best interpreted. Here, Schindler's sexuality, which has been central to the portrayal of the character, is coded as destructive. The contrast between Schindler and Goeth detailed in terms of Goeth's sadism and Schindler's acts of mercy here collapses. As Goeth says a few scenes later, arguing on behalf of Schindler, "You should have seen this girl. They put a spell on you, Jewish women." In his mind, there is no difference between the two of them.

The mood shifts dramatically in the following scenes. Schindler walks from his apartment to find a rain of ashes blotting the sun, and a pile of ash on the fender of his car. The film cuts to the Plaszow labor camp, where the bodies of 10,000 Jews killed during the liquidation and at the labor camp must be exhumed and burned. The Jewish prisoners are forced to exhume the bodies, while the Nazi soldiers supervise in a hysterical and ineffectual way. This sorrowful and harrowing scene is driven home when Schindler sees the body of the little red-coated girl being wheeled to the fire. Goeth tells him, "The party's over, Oscar. They're shipping everyone to Auschwitz." Schindler says goodbye to Stern, tells him he will move back to his hometown in Czechoslovakia, and that thanks to Stern, he has made more money than any man can spend in a lifetime. They at last have a drink together.

In the early morning hours, with a girl lightly snoring in his bed, Schindler has a change of heart, and an inspiration. As Billie Holiday plays on the phonograph, Schindler moves to the window and looks toward the future. He begins gathering all his money, distributing it among several huge suitcases. As he makes his sales pitch to Goeth, Schindler exhibits the full force of his charm. Dressed in serious business attire, a cigarette in one hand, a cognac in the other, he persuades Goeth to allow him to "buy" his Jews. "You want these people?" "My people. I want my people." Who are you, Moses?" As Stern types up the list that Schindler narrates from memory, a sense of excitement and anxiety suffuses the scene. Finally, the list is complete. Schindler instructs him to leave one space at the bottom – the space reserved for Helen Hirsch. As Schindler is shown in extreme shadow, with only a faint outline of light illuminating his profile, Stern holds up the list and says, "The list is an absolute good. The list is life. All around its margins lies the gulf."

The final act of the redemptive narrative of Oskar Schindler occurs after he has departed the scene. After rescuing 1,100 Jews from certain death at Auschwitz, Schindler brings the workers to his home town of Bresnau, Czechoslovakia. They go to work in a munitions factory he has purchased, and Stern is instructed to "never make a single shell that can be fired." Here, Schindler renews his relationship with his wife, controls the German soldiers guarding the camp, and reinstitutes the keeping of the Sabbath. After the German surrender, he will be, he tells the assembled multitude, a "wanted man. A member of the Nazi Party. A war profiteer off slave labor." He must escape at midnight, and does so in the borrowed stripes of prison-camp clothing, with his wife. The workers first present him with a ring, melted from the gold tooth of one of the workers, inscribed with the Hebrew saying from the Talmud: "Whoever saves one life, saves the world entire." This precipitates a moving, emotional scene where Schindler decries his own lack of effort, all the money he threw away, the car that he still owns that could have saved ten more Jews, and the Nazi pin he holds in his hand that could have saved one. He is chastened, humbled, and has come full circle to occupy the position of the Jews, dressed in their prison clothing, hunted.

But it is in the closing scenes and the epilogue that the film most fully articulates its reading of history and the place of Schindler's actions within it. The historical narrative of exodus and emergence is reiterated here in a few shots that dilate the realist frame of the film to connect it to the core story of Jewish history. As the Schindler Jews at the factory are "liberated" by a single Russian soldier, they are told not to go east, "They hate you there." And "don't go west either." Stern tells him they need food, and the Russian soldier points to a hill, and says, "Isn't that a town over there?" The Schindler Jews begin walking, cresting the hill in a single, long horizontal line, and the camera begins detailing their faces as they move toward the future. The epic structure here is unmistakable. The emergence of a people, the founding of a nation, the movement from persecution to freedom gives the closing moments of the film a distinctly biblical encoding, moving toward a new land, a land that Schindler cannot enter.

The final scene of the film brings the viewer into the present, and shows the surviving Schindler Jews and their offspring, accompanied by the actors who played them, filing by Schindler's tomb to each place a rock upon it. In a graphic title placed over the images, Spielberg tells us that there are only 4,000 Jews remaining in Poland, but that the descendants of the Schindler Jews number some 10,000. Schindler has become, in effect, the "father" of these 10,000. The absence of family in Schindler's life, the failure of his marriage, the failure of several subsequent business endeavors is redeemed in this final sequence. The biographical film, which so often contrasts the greatness of the man of genius with the ordinariness of his domestic life, the conflict and strain but also the homely familiarity of it, is here reiterated but inverted. The achievement of Schindler is precisely the continuation of family, a family that the film narrates as the rebirth of a nation. Rewriting the history of the Holocaust as an epic story of emergence, *Schindler's List* draws on the resources of the biographical film to invest the most horrific and momentous event of the twentieth century with a powerful message of continuity and hope.

Notes

1   Claude Lanzmann, "Why Spielberg has Distorted the Truth," *Guardian Weekly*, April 3, 1994: 14. Translated from *Le Monde*, March 3, 1994: 1, 7.

2   Elie Weisel, foreword to Annette Insdorf, *Indelible Shadows: Film and the Holocaust*, 3rd ed. (New York: Cambridge University Press, 2003): xi.

3   Art Spiegelman, *Maus I: A Survivor's Tale* (1986) and *Maus II: And Here My Troubles Began* (1991) received a special Pulitzer Prize in 1992. Roberto Benigni received three Academy Awards in 1999 for *Life is Beautiful* (1997).

4   See Miriam Bratu Hansen, "Schindler's List Is Not Shoah," *Critical Inquiry* 22 (Winter 1996): 297.

5   See Yosefa Loshitzky, "Introduction," in Loshitzky, ed., *Spielberg's Holocaust* (Bloomington: Indiana University Press, 1997): 1–17.

6   Robert Rosenstone, *History on Film/Film On History* (Harlow, England and New York: Pearson Education, 2006): 89–110.

7   Roland Barthes, quoted in ibid.: 91.

8   Hansen, "Schindler's List Is Not Shoah": 307.

9   Omer Bartov, "Spielberg's Oskar: Hollywood Tries Evil," in Loshitzky, *Spielberg's Holocaust*: 43.

10 Gary Weissman, *Fantasies of Witnessing: Postwar Efforts to Experience the Holocaust* (Ithaca, NY: Cornell University Press, 2004): 159.

11 Judith E. Doneson, "The Image Lingers: The Feminization of the Jew in *Schindler's List*," in Loshitzky, *Spielberg's Holocaust*: 146.

12 Geoffrey H. Hartman, "The Cinema Animal," in Loshitzky, *Spielberg's Holocaust*: 62.

13 George F. Custen, *Bio/Pics: How Hollywood Constructed Public History* (New York: Rutgers University Press, 1992): 19.

14 Geoffrey H. Hartman makes this point in "The Cinema Animal": 63. Slavoj Žižek quotes Himmler's speech: "a glorious day in our history, and one that has never been written and can never be written." See Žižek, *Welcome to the Desert of the Real* (London and New York: Verso, 2002): 30–1.

15 Thomas Keneally, *Schindler's List* (New York: Serpentine Publishing, 1982).

16 This theme runs through Custen's book, but is especially prominent in Chapter Five, "Configuring a Life."

16 Leo Lowenthal, "Biographies in Popular Magazines," *Radio Research: 1942–3*, ed. Paul Lazarsfeld and Frank Stanton (New York: Duell, Sloan & Pearce, 1944). Cited in Custen, *Bio/Pics*: 32–4.

17 Custen, *Bio/Pics*: 32–80.

18 Caroline Joan S. Picart and David Frank, *Frames of Evil: The Holocaust as Horror in American Film* (Carbondale: Southern Illinois University Press, 2006): 36–69.

19 Caroline Joan S. Picart and David Frank, *Frames of Evil: The Holocaust as Horror in American Film* (Carbondale: Southern Illinois University Press, 2006): 36–69.

CHAPTER 5

THE METAHISTORICAL FILM: *JFK*

In this chapter I consider Oliver Stone's *JFK* as a prototype of what Robert Rosenstone calls "a new form of history ... history as vision."[1] *JFK* constitutes a radical departure from the realist style of historical narration that has dominated Hollywood practice, presenting instead a history consisting of rapid shifts between objective and subjective images, radically disjunctive montage editing, and multiple contesting plotlines. In revising a specific interpretation of the past – an interpretation that was enabled and promoted by the mass media of the day – *JFK* provides an exemplary demonstration of a metahistorical film, a work that starts by questioning the dominant understanding of a particular event, and that challenges the way the history of that event has been written and disseminated. At the most fundamental level, *JFK* presents a provocative critique of the Warren Commission explanation of the assassination of John F. Kennedy, contesting in particular its claim that Lee Harvey Oswald acted alone in killing the president. In the film's view, the Warren Commission investigators worked in concert with the mass media to create a convenient culprit in Oswald. As *JFK* makes clear, the one piece of exculpatory evidence which would demonstrate the improbability of Oswald acting alone – the famous Zapruder film – was kept from the American public by the Time-Life Corporation for five years. The film can thus be seen as a cinematic dissection of the Warren Commission's arguments, a dissection rendered in a highly charged, polemical style that mixes idioms, splices together documentary and fictional footage, and uses montage editing to disorient and "agitate" the viewer. Its goal is to call into question what had become the official, accepted interpretation of the assassination, an interpretation that, the film argues, is riddled with inconsistencies and investigative failures, that overlooks obvious potential lead, and actively suppresses evidence. The counter-history that emerges is a dazzling experiment in film language, and a provocative example of the power of film as a medium of historical argument. It is also highly controversial, provoking difficult questions about the responsibility of historical film to the historical "record," and in particular, to the photographic archive that is becoming more and more the basis of our consensual historical reality.

Rosenstone divides historical films into three general categories: those that "vision" history, that present a traditional, experiential representation of the past in a more or less realist framework; those that "contest" history and challenge the narratives that structure historical knowledge; and those that "revision" "history," films that reject the realism that purports to show the world "as it is" in favor of "expressive modes of representation that expand the vocabulary of the historian."[2] An accomplished and controversial work, *JFK* "revisions" not only the official accounts of Kennedy's assassination, but also the traditional realism of the historical film, placing pressure on the codes and conventions by which history is represented in the cinema. Although there are strong traditions of radically innovative approaches to historical filmmaking in other national cinemas – one thinks immediately of the Soviet cinema and the New Latin American cinema – there are few examples of stylistically innovative historical films in the United States. Works such as *Walker, Zoot Suit, Courage Under Fire,* and *Three Kings* are a few of the other works that might correspond to this category.

Seen in the most positive light, *JFK* can be considered a mode of "thought experiment," a historiographic project that represents a new form of historical thinking.[3] The film foregrounds its own construction and narrates the past self-reflexively from a multiplicity of viewpoints, refusing to insist on a unified narrative trajectory or a coherent, single meaning of events. The fragmentary, postmodernist style of *JFK*, which mixes factual and fictional discourses in a speculative and critical approach to the past, challenges the realist tradition that has dominated historical filmmaking in the United States, and can instead be compared to postmodern practices in fiction, music, poetry, and painting. In particular, Stone's technique of sampling the documentary archive of photographs, newsreels, recorded speeches, and written documents draws on the vocabulary of postmodernism, a style marked by ironic quotation and pastiche. In Stone's hands, the documentary record becomes subject to a radical scrutiny, as the powerful images broadcast by the media are quoted, seamlessly woven together with staged footage, recombined with other media forms, and placed in new contexts.

Viewed from a different, more negative perspective, however, *JFK* violates many of the central tenets of historical representation. It fuses together documentary and fictional footage in a way that is designed to blur the boundaries between them, and presents highly speculative sequences in what appears to be a documentary format, making it difficult for the viewer to distinguish between actual documentary footage and fictional re-creation.

One of the questions I will consider in this chapter is whether JFK can be understood as a new form of historical thinking. Can Stone's filmmaking be considered a form of historiography suitable for a post-literate age, as some critics have argued? And further, is the authenticity of any particular piece of data less significant than the overall truth of the argument? Many historians and commentators on the film argue strongly from the opposite position, maintaining that *JFK* violates norms and standards of historical interpretation to the extent that it cannot be considered a form of historical inquiry, that it represents media culture at its most irresponsible. Rosenstone summarizes this issue by asking if the new visual and acoustic vocabulary of historical film calls for a different sense of truth and authenticity than that of written history. The ascendancy of the visual media, he writes, constitutes a major shift in historical consciousness, a shift that is equivalent to the dramatic changes that occurred when oral history and storytelling gave way to written accounts. Can a metaphoric or symbolic truth, a poetic truth, similar to that of oral history, he asks, take precedence over specific items of data and documentation?[4] In this chapter, I will return to issues of historical representation and film that I considered more generally at the beginning of this book, with specific consideration of the borderline between fiction and documentary evidence and the issue of historical responsibility in film.

The release of *JFK* created a furor among historians, journalists, and political commentators. The attacks on the film actually began some six months before its release, when a journalist, George Lardner, Jr., allegedly received a bootleg copy of the draft script. Roughly based on the story of Jim Garrison, a New Orleans District Attorney who brought the only prosecution in the JFK assassination, the script of JFK made Garrison an idealized figure and ignored his questionable tactics, such as hypnotizing witnesses. Lardner, writing for *The Washington Post*, had witnessed parts of the Garrison proceedings against Clay Shaw, and found that the case was full of flaws. He attacked Stone for using the Garrison investigation, and the subsequent book by Garrison *On the Trail of the Assassins*, as the basis of his film, calling it "a fraud." Titling his article "Dallas in Wonderland," Lardner claimed the script was also full of errors and "absurdities."[5]

Upon its release, the film was denounced by many of the leading cultural commentators in the United States, and was the subject of highly unusual front-page attacks by the editorial writers for the *New York Times*. It should be noted, however, that the *New York Times* was the publisher of the Warren Commission Report, and thus had a significant investment in its remaining the accepted historical record of the assassination. The reaction to the film among political commentators and talk-show figures was widespread and negative. George Will, a well-known conservative commentator, wrote that "*JFK* is an act of execrable history . . . In this three-hour lie, Stone falsifies so much that he may be an intellectual sociopath, indifferent to truth." Alexander Cockburn, an influential left-wing commentator, was almost as extreme, writing that Stone's "history is bogus and his aesthetics questionable." *Newsweek* ran a cover story about the film, emblazoned with the words: "The Twisted Truth of 'JFK': Why Oliver Stone's New Movie Can't Be Trusted." Hodding Carter, a former press secretary for President Jimmy Carter, in a particularly colorful quote, said the film contained "countless buckets of manure, large measures of legitimate doubt, drippings of innuendo and pages of actual history." Anthony Lewis of the *New York Times* called the treatment of Earl Warren "contemptible." David Belin, a Warren Commission junior lawyer writing in the *New York Times Magazine*, titled his essay "The Big Lies of *JFK*." One commentator called JFK "the cinematic equivalent of rape."[6]

Many professional historians were outraged as well, including Thomas Reeves, who says, in his review for the *Journal of American History*, that "there is an intense hatred of the United States" evident in the view of the nation set forth by *JFK*, which argues that corruption and conspiracy exists at the highest level of the US government.[7] By contrast, however, many in the scholarly community have been willing to give Stone's work a more balanced hearing. Oliver Stone was invited to address the American Historical Society in 1997, and he accepted the invitation to defend his work and his historical approach to a professional audience. The success of that conference resulted in a major publication,

Oliver Stone's USA: Film, History, and Controversy, which contains numerous essays that assess Stone's entire *oeuvre* in terms of historical accuracy, politics, and his image of nation. Perhaps most valuable is the fact that Stone responds in the volume to each of these essays in a detailed and convincing fashion. Perhaps the most generous and positive assessment of Stone's work by a historian is that of Rosenstone: "whatever its flaws, *JFK* has to be among the most important works of American history ever to appear on the screen."[8] For his part, Oliver Stone published a 700-page work, *JFK: The Book of the Film*, which includes several new essays, both pro and con, an annotated script, and numerous supporting documents. Here, nearly every line of dialogue in the film is scrupulously annotated, thoroughly documenting the source material for the arguments the characters express. It is a massive, exhaustively referenced and cross-referenced work that lends a good deal of authority to Stone's version of the events. The book of the film, while including much of the most scathing criticism of the work, effectively refutes the charge that the film is pure paranoid speculation, demonstrating in its detail and its spirit of open inquiry that the film in fact offers a plausible interpretation of the past.

Kurtz writes that "with the exception of *Uncle Tom's Cabin . . . JFK* probably had a greater impact on public opinion than any other work of art in American history."[9] The interest generated by *JFK* resulted in a new government investigation and public hearings in the spring and summer of 1992, where it was revealed that there was indeed a cover-up and suppression of millions of pages of evidence relating to the assassination. The "President John F. Kennedy Records Collection Act of 1992" was the result, which called for the collection and release of all assassination records. The final report by the commission placed in charge of this process credited *JFK* with creating the public pressure that led to the legislation. The documents released by the commission reveal numerous instances of suppression, tampering, and falsifying of evidence. As Kurtz writes, "for all of *JFK*'s faults and shortcomings, few producers and directors can claim such an impact from their movies, and few historians can claim such an impact from their works."[10]

Narrative Strategies

The controversies associated with *JFK* revolve around the narrative framework of the film, its focus on Jim Garrison, and on the formal innovations of the work, in particular the radical mixing of fictional and documentary scenes. The accelerated editing and extraordinary mixing of film idioms in *JFK* is counterbalanced, however, by the familiar contours of the narrative of Jim Garrison, portrayed here by Kevin Costner as a kind of Everyman in search of justice. Garrison, Stone has written, is a kind of emblem of the American people, less a specific character than an allegory of the nation in general. Troubled by what might be a New Orleans connection to the assassination, by the presence in New Orleans of a shady and unsavory character named David Ferrie, who was in some obscure way linked to the events in Dallas, Garrison begins reading the Warren Commission Report, and begins noticing a number of inconsistencies and potential leads that were not followed up. As he begins interviewing people, the name Clay Shaw keeps coming up in connection with radical right-wing elements in New Orleans. Ultimately, Garrison connects the name Clay Shaw to Lee Harvey Oswald. As his investigation gains momentum, Garrison is subjected to persecution in the press, wiretaps, FBI investigations, attempted frames, and veiled threats against his family. His investigation becomes compromised by a staff member, who has been intimidated by the FBI, and infiltrated by numerous "volunteers" working for the government. In the end, the prosecution of Shaw is not successful, despite vivid and convincing evidence of a cover-up. The film ends with Garrison making an impassioned summation to the courtroom audience, finally turning directly to the camera, and saying to the film's audience, "It's up to you."

For many political commentators, however, the most vulnerable point in the film is precisely the weakness of Garrison's legal investigation and the sensational nature of the case against New Orleans businessman Shaw, whom Garrison accused of being a conspirator in the assassination. Garrison's case against Shaw had been roundly criticized for its reliance on supposedly questionable witnesses, thin evidence, and wild speculation. Kurtz writes that "Garrison's arrogance and pomposity, his cryptic remarks to the press that the truth about the assassination was lurking 'behind the looking glass,' and his railroading of uncooperative witnesses . . . have been thoroughly examined."[11] However, Stone makes the striking point that the case had gone before a grand jury, which issued an indictment, that a total of twenty-two jurors had heard the evidence and that at a preliminary hearing a three-judge panel had ruled that there was enough evidence to go to trial.[12] Moreover, the jury at the trial all said that "they believed there had been a conspiracy to kill JFK, but that the evidence was not sufficient to convict Clay Shaw." Perhaps most importantly, Garrison was the first person to bring the famous Zapruder film – the 8mm film of the assassination taken by Abraham

Zapruder – to the public eye. It had been sequestered by Time-Life Corporation for five years after the assassination, and never seen by the public until the trial of Clay Shaw. From a political and historical perspective, the Shaw trial represented a valuable advance in our knowledge of the assassination.

Stone has said that the Garrison played by Kevin Costner is a kind of idealized archetype, an Everyman in pursuit of justice similar to the hero of a Frank Capra film. Garrison's family life, his warm relations with his staff, and his homespun innocence are set off against the radical discontinuity of the film's style, serving as a rhetorical container that brings the drama of the film into personal, individual focus. The grounding of its innovative visual and acoustic style in an individual quest for justice, however, also serves a significant formal and narrative purpose. By focalizing the investigation and the theory of the assassination through an individual character, the powerful pseudo-documentary sequences that fill the film are rendered mainly as individual hypotheses, speculative possibilities, filtered through the mindscreen of an individual character. Thus the scenes of President Lyndon Johnson's shadowy conversations, the sinister passages detailing the movements of several assassins in Dallas, the placing of the "magic bullet" on a stretcher in the Dallas morgue, the exchange of glances between Lee Harvey Oswald and Jack Ruby just before Oswald is shot – are rendered as hypotheses, possibilities that are imagined or presented as the mindscreen of the characters rather than as the "facts" of the fictional world.

Individual, personal narration in film and in literature has a different narrative status than impersonal, third-person narration. For one thing, it is not "predicated," that is, personal narration does not comprise the "facts" of the story-world, the elements that are understood as "true" and "consistent" in the fictional universe.[13] This is a central but little-understood structural characteristic of narrative form. The individual character-narrator – for example, as in *The Usual Suspects* – may provide a "personal" narrative of events which may even be illustrated by images and scenes. As the camera returns to the source of the story – the narrative told by the main character in the police station – we are reminded that this is simply his version of the facts, a story concocted on the spot, but which seemed authentic to the audience because it is visualized as if they were scenes from the character's memory. Personal narration simply does not carry the veridical value, the truth value, of third-person impersonal narration. Personal narrators can lie, invent, or embellish. And personal narration can be illustrated by images that "lie," as occurs in *The Usual Suspects*, and also, famously, in Alfred Hitchcock's

Stage Fright, where the "lying narrator's" fabrications are illustrated by dramatic scenes.

In the case of *JFK*, nearly all of the most controversial scenes of pseudo-documentary events unfold under the sign of personal narration. This is not to suggest that these sequences should be considered visual "lies," but rather that they unfold under an explicit narrative indication that they are speculative and hypothetical, that they are scenarios of what *may* have occurred. The great majority of the speculative sequences that have created so much controversy in the film are introduced with statements to the effect of "What if it happened this way?" or "Perhaps this is what occurred?" Other speculative scenes are conveyed as the illustrated personal testimony of the various witnesses Garrison interviews in his investigation. The pseudo-documentary sequences, with very few exceptions, are examples of personal narration illustrated in a documentary style. As we know from the famous example of the Akira Kurosawa film, *Rashomon*, personal narration conveys only a version of events, a version that is not meant to be seen as definitive.

JFK's narrative style, its unusual and innovative mixture of personal and impersonal narration, of speculation and actual documentary imagery, in some cases spliced together, explodes the conventions of the traditional Hollywood historical film. *JFK* weaves a history of what might have occurred into the fabric of what actually did occur. For Stone, this "revisioning" of history is essential, a counterweight to the falsification of history presented by the government and the media. Stone writes: "We are all victims of counterfeit history. In my lifetime I have learned this lesson by head and by heart . . . *never underestimate the power of corruption to rewrite history.*"[14]

The multiple layers of fiction, reality, and supposition create an intricate texture, a web of correspondences and associations whose cumulative effect has been described by Roger Ebert as "hypnotic." What in French critical circles is called the "écriture" of the film, the "filmic writing," is exceptionally nuanced and intricate here. Rosenstone suggests that JFK may be a precursor of the history of the future, a text that synthesizes an extraordinary number of visual and acoustic forms in the service of an elusive and complex argument. In what follows, I will analyze several sequences in detail in order to consider and assess *JFK*'s historiographic strategies, which can be characterized, in my view, as an attempt to render what the historian R. L. Collingwood calls the "inside" of historical events.[15]

The beginning of the film functions as a prologue: President Dwight D. Eisenhower is shown on television giving his "Farewell Address," warning about the rapidly escalating power of the "military-industrial complex." The film then presents a history of the late 1950s and early 1960s rendered in short, fragmentary sequences linked together by voice-over and different musical motifs. The opening montage is a work of assemblage, combining footage from grainy newsreels, television advertising of the period, home movies, still photographs from magazines, "library" footage of churchgoing, missile launches, family picnics, and television newscasts. John F. Kennedy is here portrayed in footage drawn from newsreels and home movies as a confident, capable leader, charismatic and grounded in the political realities of the period. He is also portrayed as open to cooperation with the Soviet Union, and thus threatening to the military-industrial complex Eisenhower had identified in his Farewell Address. Secret wars, assassinations, coups d'état, the civil rights struggle, and nuclear threats are also conveyed, resulting in a montage that creates a vivid and compelling portrait of the period. The ominous future portended by these images is set against the promise of a new kind of government, embodied in the person of Kennedy. The sequence conveys a powerful impression of two nations, two Americas coexisting in one historical period – a fresh, confident young nation oriented to the future, shadowed by a militaristic, predatory nation of plots and counterplots defined by the ideology of the Cold War.

The macro-textual composition of the prologue, which begins directly after Eisenhower's speech, is organized into four segments. After Eisenhower's address, which is the first part of the prologue, the film begins with a montage summary of the world Kennedy will enter, a world dominated by Cold War ideology, threats to America's business interests in Cuba and other Latin American countries, and images of a complacent country largely oblivious to the threats looming both within and without. Following this is a sequence, the third segment, devoted to Kennedy's campaign and inauguration, scenes that underscore the youth and energy of Kennedy and his "beautiful young wife." Kennedy's inauguration and a summary of his short presidency follow, a black-and-white sequence that contrasts Kennedy's role in Washington and the larger geopolitical world with color sequences illustrating his family life and moments of relaxation. Finally, the prologue shifts into another montage style to depict the fateful motorcade in Dallas on November 22, 1963, ending with a black screen and the sound of a rifle being cocked.

Eisenstein has said that conflict is the nerve of the cinema. Conflict in shot size, screen direction, color, movement, texture, and sound

dominates the sequence, creating a kind of polyphonic effect: the spectator not only "sees" and "hears" the opening montage, but more importantly, "feels" it emotionally. The root cause of Kennedy's assassination,
the sequence suggests, is the threat he poses to the business interests
profiting from the proliferating military build-up of the Cold War, a
build-up that Kennedy promises to end with a new spirit of cooperation. The prologue to the film samples Kennedy's speech to American
University, in which he states his belief in the power of cooperation
with hostile governments: "What kind of world do we seek? Not a
'Pax Americana'"; it includes images of his speech to the nation about
civil rights during the Birmingham, Alabama conflict; his famous visit
to the Berlin Wall, in which he proclaims that the proudest words one
can utter are "I am a Berliner!"; his call for a unified space program
with the Soviet Union, and his initiatives with Khrushchev to sign the
Nuclear Peace Treaty of July 1963.

Although criticized for his idealistic portrait of Kennedy in *JFK*, Stone
says that the image of Kennedy he conveys here is the Kennedy of
that period, a "television story," the official portrait of the Kennedy
"we knew at the time."[16] In counterpoint, however, the antipathy Kennedy
had generated in the South for his Civil Rights endeavors, and the
clashes between Kennedy and the CIA, the FBI, and other secretive
organizations within the government is established as well. The turbul-
ence of the period is captured in violent images of beatings, attack
dogs, missiles, explosions, and fiery rallies, while the tranquil prospect
of a new Camelot is captured in color photography of Kennedy with
his wife and family.

By analyzing one microtextual sequence of four shots, we can begin
to appreciate the subtlety and effectiveness of Stone's montage practice.
The sequence I have in mind occurs approximately halfway through
the prologue. Allen Dulles, the Director of the CIA, is being described
on the soundtrack as masterminding a secret plot to overthrow Castro,
keeping Kennedy out of the loop. In the visuals, Dulles is seen offering his hand to Kennedy as they are both standing outside the White
House for a photo op. Kennedy pretends not to see him, and turns
away. The next two shots are violent scenes picturing the captured Cuban
rebels, one being kicked in the head, another being dragged away. The
soundtrack is dominated by an ominous ticking sound and deep bass
drum. The sequence then returns to Kennedy, who looks back at Dulles,
whose hand has been withdrawn. The two men then awkwardly come
together for a handshake. The short sequence communicates Kennedy's
distrust of Dulles, the reasons for the distrust, and subtly connotes a

message that Dulles has "blood on his hands." An ordinary news shot of Dulles and Kennedy, insignificant and unremarkable on its own, is here broken up into two shots with violent images inserted in between. The sequence illustrates Eisenstein's view that the contrast and collision of shots is the key to cinematic meaning, creating messages that cannot be found in the individual shots themselves.

Here, Stone uses the media images of the day as a tool to dissect the secret life of the nation's power structure, the inner life of America's past, what Collingwood calls the "inside of history." Intriguingly, Stone argues that the media became the dominant force in American culture precisely on the day of Kennedy's assassination: "It seems that we all saw it one way – the way it was so confidently told to us by 'the Media,' which leapt into major prominence in our public consciousness as an *entity* that fateful day."[17]

The sampling and repurposing of media footage and documentary imagery is also the primary source of the fourth segment of the prologue – the shots of Kennedy's arrival in Dallas and the motorcade approaching and entering Dealey Plaza. Contrast and collision characterize this sequence, which include numerous shots of the motorcade, of spectators lining the streets, protest signs excoriating Kennedy, young families cheering the president, and periodic shots of a large clock atop a building digitally counting the minutes. The shot composition follows the principles of metric montage, shots of uniform length that are cut together without regard to content. Metric montage, which Eisenstein defined as the simplest type, conveys a sense of inevitability, the mechanical working out of a predetermined plan. Augmenting this impression are the resonant tympani and military snare drum driving the soundtrack. The syncopated march rhythm seems to reinforce the metric cutting, but the contrasts between movement within the shot and the movement of the camera, between near and far, color and black-and-white, moving and still, create a sense of agitation and unease. Many of the shots used in this sequence are documentary images of the Kennedy motorcade, although some are re-creations. Finally, as Kennedy's limousine enters Elm Street, and he pushes his hair back in a familiar gesture and waves to the crowd, the screen goes black, the sound of a rifle cocking is heard, and a shot rings out. We next see a view of the Texas Book Depository roof where a flock of birds takes flight. Following this, we see the beginnings of the television announcement of Kennedy's shooting and a blurry segment from the Zapruder film showing Jackie Kennedy crawling back onto the trunk of the limousine to alert the Secret Service that her husband has been shot.

Consensual Reality and Speculative History

The prologue of the film follows a straightforward time-line, a cause-and-effect logic, employing media imagery and documentary footage to sketch the beginnings of its counter-history. Limiting itself to documentary images sorted and arranged in a vivid and disjunctive way, the prologue nevertheless makes a strong suggestion concerning the reasons for Kennedy's assassination: Kennedy's death resulted from his new moves toward cooperation and accommodation with Cold War enemies, his moves toward an ideology of peaceful coexistence threatening many powerful people invested in the Cold War. The voice-over by Martin Sheen is limited to a factual narrative about the events of the day; along with quotes from unnamed sources such as "rumors abound that Kennedy is 'soft on communism.'" The motorcade itself is introduced by a short, haunting sequence of shots involving a woman named Rose Charamaine, a prostitute and drug runner who, while in hospital two days before the assassination, warned the staff and all who would listen that "They're going to kill Kennedy. In Dallas. These are serious fucking guys! Help!" A kind of Cassandra figure, her voice echoes on the soundtrack as the film switches to documentary images of Kennedy's plane landing in Dallas.

The film's use of documentary footage in the opening prologue provides an image of a reality that is shared and consensual. Although the documentary images are arranged to serve the purpose of exposition and suggestion, the images are drawn from the archives of the wider media culture. *Time Magazine*, newscasts, home movies: these are the sources, Stone implies, of our consensual reality. But the main focus of the film is to blur the line between this consensual reality and the speculative history the film sets forth. From this point forward, the film moves on to the depiction of a reality that is prismatic and contradictory, that weaves fact and fiction together, and that constructs a counter-history out of all the cinematic means available.

Garrison is introduced directly after the sequence from the Zapruder film that concludes the prologue. The opening sequences featuring Garrison serve the dual purpose of sketching the communal reaction to Kennedy's death and introducing Garrison in the context of his milieu: the well-known New Orleans restaurant, Napoleon's, where he watches the initial broadcast announcing Kennedy's death; his family dining room, where he watches the broadcast announcing Oswald's arrest as a prime suspect in the shooting of Officer J. D. Tippitt and as a primary suspect in the Kennedy assassination; and in his office together

FIGURE 5.1 "One of the grossest lies ever forced upon the American people, we've come to know it as the 'magic bullet' theory." Jim Garrison (Kevin Costner) reconstructs the murder of President John F. Kennedy in *JFK* (1991) [Warner Brothers/Photofest]

with his staff. The consensual reality of the nation is associated strongly here with the media's power to communicate an instantaneous judgment, a power to fashion a version of reality that is almost universal in its reach.

In the first sequence featuring Oswald, which Garrison watches at home with his family on the night of the assassination, Stone cuts into the broadcast of archival footage to present Gary Oldman's uncannily realistic impersonation of Oswald, making statements about his innocence to reporters as he is led away in handcuffs. The combination of staged material and archival footage is not seamless, but it is effective in conveying an impression of reality. Although Stone's pseudo-documentary sequences have been the subject of a great deal of criticism, the criticism has not taken into account his powerful attempt to deconstruct the media reality that has become the basis of collective judgment in the nation. On the one hand, it can be argued that the film tries to break through the media's grip on consciousness by interweaving speculative, dramatic shots into actual media footage, creating a powerful method of deconstructing the theater of reality that the media presents. The weaving together of actual footage and staged scenes in the same footage may be seen as a powerfully innovative tool; Stone has said that historical film should try to break through the three dimensions of everyday reality by using every tool at its disposal. On the other hand, the interpolation of staged shots into archival footage may be seen as a manipulation of data that confirms the most negative appraisals of Stone as a deceptive purveyor of paranoid fantasies and half-truths.

In the digital culture of the present, the manipulation of documentary images and sounds is omnipresent; films such as *Wag the Dog* and *Forrest Gump* have satirized the concept of an inherent truth value or authenticity in the images broadcast by the mass media, or the images that are seen to comprise our collective historical record. The use of documentary techniques to stage fictional scenes has been well-known since the film *The Battle of Algiers*, which uses a documentary style to create a story that has no actual documentary sequences in it. Nevertheless, there remains a kind of aura of authenticity that surrounds the genre of documentary filmmaking, and it is this aura or residue of authenticity that has made *JFK* a particularly controversial text.

Many historical films employ documentary images or texts as authenticating devices, using fragments of newsreels or pseudo-newsreels in the course of the film to create an impression of authenticity. In some earlier films, scenes are staged as "exact facsimiles" of the actual event, as in the Lincoln assassination scene in *The Birth of a Nation*. Intended to demonstrate the "bona fides" of the historical film, these "documentary" passages are often set apart from the rest of the film, underlined by the filmmaker as evidence of their good faith in presenting an accurate version of the past. The use of documentary images in historical fiction films cuts both ways, however, for by foregrounding the authenticity of the fragment, it also calls attention to the constructed nature of the overall story.

Functioning almost as a certificate of authenticity, the documentary or pseudo-documentary sequence suggests that there is a relation of continuity between the fictional, dramatic narrative unfolding on the screen and the actual historical events it purports to represent. *JFK* employs this very type of authenticating discourse in its powerful use of the Zapruder film, which Stone asserts is not manipulated in any way. Stone inserts short fragments of the Zapruder film in various sequences, and renders it in its entirety during the climactic trial scene, where the "visual evidence" of the direction of the fatal shot is stressed. However, the overall message that emerges from *JFK*'s use of embedded documentary sequences is somewhat more complicated. We have already discussed the prologue of the film and its montage technique, its recutting and recombining of media images from the past. The creative use of montage here suggests that montage editing can reveal the inside of historical events, the inner truth, comparable to Eisenstein's belief that montage could reveal historical dialectics at work. In two major scenes that represent the assassination of Lee Harvey Oswald, however, Stone goes a step further, splicing together actual documentary footage and staged sequences. Combining documentary images and staged footage, the event of Oswald's murder becomes extraordinarily vivid and dramatic. But another message emerges as well, one that subtly insinuates a connection, a subterranean complicity among the figures in the sequence.

Stone represents the killing of Lee Harvey Oswald twice, once at the beginning of the film soon after Garrison is introduced, and once during the trial of Clay Shaw. In both representations, actual footage is used at various points in combination with staged shots. In the first representation, Garrison is sitting in his office with his associates, watching television as Oswald is brought down to the parking garage from his holding cell in the Dallas Police Department. All eyes are on the

FIGURE 5.2 Lee Harvey Oswald (Gary Oldman) is shot by Jack Ruby in the basement of the Dallas Police Station. *JFK* (1991). [Warner Brothers/Photofest]

television, as we first see what Garrison and his associates see: blurred, grainy black-and-white television footage of Oswald being brought into the parking garage. The camera then cuts to a series of staged medium close-ups and reverse angles, photographed in a more vivid, crisp black and white, depicting Oswald walking in the garage and Jack Ruby standing in the crowd. As Ruby makes his move toward Oswald, shouting "Oswald!," the scene cuts back to the actual archival footage of Oswald being shot in the gut. Next, Oswald is seen lying on the floor of the garage, first in a staged shot, followed by a shot from the actual footage. The sequence ends with a series of staged shots that show Oswald being carried on a stretcher and placed in an ambulance, with one of these shots coming from the actual archival footage.

In the second representation of this event, Stone interpolates several more images, using more stylized imagery. Beginning the sequence with archival footage, as before, Stone now introduces a series of eyeline matches between Oswald and Ruby, rendered in powerful and haunting slow motion. As Ruby shoots Oswald, fast-motion camerawork is used, and the archival shot of the actual shooting is inserted. Then, as Oswald slumps to the floor in a staged shot in extreme slow motion, Stone inserts a series of reaction shots to various onlookers, who seem to express no surprise or shock, but rather a kind of knowing satisfaction.

The psychological dimension that is introduced here, as Oswald and Ruby are given the kind of close-up portraiture and eyeline connection that imply subjectivity, orients the historical events of Oswald's murder in the direction of conspiracy: Stone imaginatively "enters" the scene of Oswald's murder, rethinks it, presents it from a psychological perspective and defamiliarizes images long established as part of the historical archive. Oswald's murder now has a subtle but distinct new message attached to it, a message concerning the strong possibility of a conspiracy, of a connection between Oswald and Ruby that has turned fatal for Oswald. Coming as it does during the trial of Clay Shaw, the audience is well prepared to accept this interpretation.[18]

The cinematic rewriting of the historical past is here pushed to the level of the historical documents themselves. The audiovisual archive of American history in the twentieth century is quoted, reimagined, and reinterpreted through the use of cinematic techniques that make it difficult to distinguish between archival footage and dramatic interpretation. Stone has said that

> the style of my films is ambivalent and shifting. I make people aware that they are watching a movie. I make them aware that reality itself is

in question . . . the movie is not only about a conspiracy to kill President Kennedy, but also about the way we look at our recent history. [*JFK*] calls attention to itself as a means of looking at history – shifting styles, such as the use of black and white and color, and viewing people from offbeat angles.[19]

Although Stone is careful not to alter or tamper with the documentary images themselves, his imaginative quoting and re-presentation of the audiovisual documents, rapidly splicing in staged footage, repurposes the archival material. Blurring the line between documentary and fiction, Stone practices a form of radical pastiche, taking snippets from the image bank of twentieth-century culture and drawing new meaning from them, imagining the "inside" of the historical event in order to create what he calls a counter-myth to the myth of the Warren Commission Report.

In doing so, Stone raises major questions about the historical past, but he also raises major questions about his own historical practice. Although the sequences of Oswald's murder have not been singled out by critics of the film, these scenes bring the issue of the mixing of fact and fiction to the forefront in a way that cannot be easily resolved through appeals to narrative theory or to postmodern aesthetics. On the negative side of the argument, we can raise the following:

1   Stone calls for full disclosure of the documents relating to the assassination; at the same time, however, he muddies the waters when it comes to the visual documents, making it hard to discern the distinction between authentic documentary images and fictional images.
2   Archival images function as certificates of authenticity, a testament of reality. The truth value associated with these images constitutes a kind of social contract. The external truth value associated with archival images is here used as a credential for the staged sequences.
3   The film implies, through its mixing of documentary and fictional sequences, that there is an equivalence between historical documents and historical interpretation. The distinction between document and interpretation is not clearly drawn.

The objections above are focused on the media and on film as a mode of historical documentation; more broadly, they touch on the larger issues of historical representation that have circulated around Stone's work. Films such as *JFK* and *Nixon* challenge accepted historical interpretation by using the medium of film in a new way, making visual arguments that seem to be burned directly into the consciousness of the viewer. The historical film thus becomes a type of cinematic rewriting of history, an assault on long-standing traditions of historical scholarship.

Several leading historians, however, including Hayden White and Rosenstone, have argued that Stone's approach to the historical past heralds a new kind of historical thinking, a modernist mode in which the past is represented in fragmented story lines, disjunctive relations of cause and effect, and in terms of compound contexts and over-lapping possibilities. Conventional history, White argues, is modeled on nineteenth-century forms, in which there is a clear-cut relation between cause and effect, a defined set of agents and patients, and a certain closure at the end. But this is not the way the monumental, catastrophic events of the twentieth century can best be addressed. White has suggested that the overwhelming, traumatic nature of historical events in the twen-tieth century, such as the Holocaust, World War II, the Great Depression, and the assassination of Kennedy, can best be represented in a modernist fashion, where the multiple strands and ambiguous causes of past events can be reflected in the form of the historical account. In his view, *JFK* heralds a type of historical practice that manifests in its formal design a modernist style of historiography that acknowledges the impossibility of mastering the historical past.[20]

Following this, the three issues I raised above might be addressed in the following ways:

1 Stone's film succeeded in making available millions of pages of formerly suppressed documents, bringing the assassination and the possibility of a cover-up into mainstream consciousness. The Warren Commission Report opts for a simple cause-and-effect narrative – a lone assassin, a single causative act, a clear-cut ending in Oswald's death. But the film's "muddying of the waters" succeeded in gen-erating an enormous release of information, placing the story line of the Warren Commission in doubt.

2 The "certificate of authenticity" associated with archival images is illusory. The media creates a consensual social reality by fore-grounding certain images and suppressing others. The film ques-tions the reality that the media chooses to purvey.

3 Documents from the past are always used by historians as part of an explanation and interpretation. They come to us embedded in a con-text. *JFK* uses documents as part of an interpretation that is explicitly stated, and in that regard uses documents in a transparent way.

Beyond the issues raised by its interpretation of the Kennedy assassination, *JFK* brings into relief fundamental issues of historical inquiry and representation. The film makes a powerful case that in the contemporary media age, historical analysis must begin with an interrogation of the images that have defined our social reality. In sequences such as the prologue, with its incisive montage of media images, and the murder of Oswald, with its interweaving of documentary and staged footage, the film conveys a sense of the influence and power of the images that define so much of twentieth-century history. Its goal is to create a counter-myth of history, a multilevel past, chaotic and ambiguous, but one that nevertheless conveys a strong sense of the moral lessons to be learned from the past.

Revisioning the Past

Certain media images possess a special status, however, and Stone reserves their use for key moments in the text. The Zapruder footage, for example, seems to haunt the film, obsessively recurring in bits and pieces throughout the work. Stone has called the Kennedy assassination our national taboo, "like Oedipus to the Greeks," and the Zapruder film serves in a sense as the moment of truth that exposes a whole secret history, the repressed core of a national trauma that only intermittently flashes into consciousness.[21] Images from the Zapruder film break into the text, for example, during Garrison's fever dream when he begins researching the Warren Commission Report. They appear at the beginning of the film in the depiction of the motorcade. And they appear in a particularly powerful montage when Garrison and his associate attempt to reproduce the alleged marksmanship of Oswald from the sixth-floor window of the Book Depository.

In this scene, Garrison and his associate station themselves at the window and attempt to visualize the event. As they discuss the direction of the motorcade, the angle of sight, the mechanical limitations of the rifle, and the documented mediocrity of Oswald's marksmanship, the film illustrates their analysis with inserts of black-and-white and color footage that bring the discussion into vivid focus. Garrison then takes the rifle in his hands and takes aim at the imaginary motorcade. In a quick and powerful montage that illustrates Garrison's visualization of the events, we see shots of the motorcade passing below, images of various bystanders, and quick, frightening black-and-white close-up shots of two additional shooters interspersed with shots of Garrison with the

FIGURE 5.3 Jim Garrison (Kevin Costner) and Lou Ivon (Jay O. Sanders) rehearse the extraordinary feat of marksmanship attributed to Lee Harvey Oswald from the sixth-floor window of the Book Depository. *JFK* (1991) [Warner Brothers/Photofest]

gun; grim and determined faces, their eyes sighting along the barrels of their rifles. Garrison's associate tells him "it takes skill to kill with a rifle, Chief. Patience. You have to figure that's why no president has been shot with one in over 100 years." These words echo strangely on the soundtrack, with the words "100 years" sounding three times in faint repetition. Garrison takes aim with the rifle, points it directly at the camera, the hammer snaps down, and the film inserts a terrifying clip from the Zapruder film showing Jackie Kennedy climbing onto the back of the limousine, accompanied by the sound of shrieking.

The Zapruder film is visualized in its entirety only during the trial of Clay Shaw, as if the threads and filaments of a traumatic scene, the fragments of a traumatic past, were now finally being given a full and complete recounting. During the film's rendition of the trial sequence, Garrison screens the film repeatedly for the jury in order to make one major point: that Kennedy's head snapped "back and to the left" with the impact of the bullet. Seen in close-up and in slow motion, the effect of the sequence is devastating. Here, Stone suggests, the visual evidence "speaks for itself." A product of a first-hand witnessing of the event, the Zapruder film here carries a status different than that of the media images Stone has sampled throughout the film. The close-up cine-matography and the slow-motion sequencing, coupled with the repetition of the critical head shot, heighten the effect of the footage. Stone, however, has said that "I didn't play with the Zapruder film, whatever critics said. It is shown exactly as it is, and it is also slowed down."[22]

The staging of this sequence is especially effective, with the projector flashing images on the screen as if the apparatus itself, the projector and the screen, were a force of revelation. The Latin American filmmakers Solanas and Gettino have called the projector a "gun that shoots twenty-four times a second," and in this sequence the power of this description is made plain. Delivering the images with minimal commentary, the film reminds us of the indexical relation to reality that defined concepts of cinema in a pre-digital age. The trauma of Kennedy's assassination is now registered in the witnessing of the act itself, the historical document serving as indexical proof, as another theorist once said, "truth at twenty-four frames per second."

These few frames from Zapruder's humble film convey the paradox of *JFK*'s act of historical revisioning. On the one hand, the film's core message and visual trump card reside in its close reading of a specific document, the Zapruder film, the visible proof that the shot that killed Kennedy came from the front. On the other hand, the splicing together of documentary and fictional sequences elsewhere in the film stresses that historical truth lies somewhere beneath the documents, between the lines, "in the wind," as one character says. *JFK* threads images from the Zapruder film into the text as a kind of touchstone of authenticity, a holy relic of the actual past, a revelation that recalls André Bazin's comparison of the photographic image to a kind of "Shroud of Turin." However, the continuous reworking, sampling, and repurposing of documentary images elsewhere in the film asserts that images do not reflect or represent the real so much as they in large part constitute it. The remedy or antidote, Stone's film argues, is to answer one constructed version of reality with another, an alternative version, a revisioning of the past.

This advanced and sophisticated conception of the relation between history and moving photographic images sets the film apart. Although the basic diegetic level of the plot concentrates on Garrison's investigation and his refusal to accept the Warren Commission Report, which appears again and again in the film as the object of Garrison's critique, the film in its formal strategies conducts a larger analysis of the manu-facturing of reality by the media. History itself is here both the object of skepticism and the object of idealization. Rosenstone writes that Stone insists on the chaotic, multiple, relativistic nature of history – in essence, on the impossibility of telling the truth of the past. But this does not prevent him from going ahead and telling us stories that carry the force of truth. Indeed, more than simply storytelling, Stone uses the past for the purpose of delivering certain kinds of truths about our national life. In his insistence on the moral lessons of history, he is exceedingly traditional.[23]

In his cinematic rewriting of a discredited chapter of the historical past, Stone provides an intriguing example of the potential for film to reveal the historical past in new and unexpected ways.

Notes

1 Robert A. Rosenstone, "Introduction" to Rosenstone, ed., *Revisioning History: Film and the Construction of a New Past* (Princeton, NJ: Princeton University Press, 1995): 6.
2 Robert Rosenstone, "Oliver Stone as Historian," in Robert Brent Toplin, ed., *Oliver Stone's USA: Film, History, and Controversy* (Lawrence: University Press of Kansas, 2000): 26–39.
3 See Natalie Zemon Davis on historical film as a mode of "thought experiment," a notion she derives from Einstein, in *Slaves on Screen* (Cambridge, MA: Harvard University Press, 2000): xi.
4 Rosenstone, "Oliver Stone as Historian": 39.
5 See the illuminating work *JFK, The Book of the Film* (New York: Applause Books, 1992). All the essays quoted above are reproduced here, including George Lardner, Jr., "On the Set: Dallas in Wonderland"; Tom Wicker, "Does JFK Conspire Against Reason?"; Alexander Cockburn, "JFK and JFK"; "Anthony Lewis, JFK"; David W. Belin, "The 'Big 'Lies' of JFK." Other quoted passages are found in Michael L. Kurtz, "Oliver Stone, JFK, and History," in Robert Brent Toplin, *Oliver Stone's USA:* 169–70.
6 See Randy Roberts and David Wellky, "A Sacred Mission: Oliver Stone and Vietnam," in Toplin, *Oliver Stone's USA*: 85.
7 Thomas Reeves, review of *JFK, Journal of American History* 79(3) (December 1992): 1263–4.
8 Rosenstone, quoted in Kurtz, "Oliver Stone, JFK, and History": 172.
9 Kurtz, "Oliver Stone, JFK, and History": 174.
10 Ibid.: 177.
11 Ibid.: 171.
12 Oliver Stone, "On Nixon and JFK," in Toplin, *Oliver Stone's USA*: 273.
13 See my essay, "The Cinematic Narrator: The Logic and Pragmatics of Impersonal Narration," *Journal of Film and Video* 42(1) (spring 1990): 3–16 for a detailed explanation of the "truth value" of fictional discourse. For

a summary, see Robert Stam, Robert Burgoyne, and Sandy Flitterman-Lewis, *New Vocabularies in Film Semiotics* (London and New York, Routledge, 1992).

14 Oliver Stone, "Stone on Stone's Image," in Toplin, *Oliver Stone's USA*: 58.

15 In *The Reality of the Historical Past*, Paul Ricoeur discusses R. L. Collingwood's work in ways that especially pertinent to Oliver Stone's endeavor in *JFK*:

> The notion of documentary proof . . . refers directly to the problem that concerns us, that of knowledge through traces. Of what exactly are documents the trace? Essentially, of the "inside" of events, which has to be called *thought*. . . . action is the union of the inside and the outside of an event. This is why the historian is the one who is obliged to 'think himself into the action, to discern the thought of its agent. (Ricoeur, quoting Collingwood, *The Idea of History*: 213)

For this example, and many other fascinating ideas on historical reenactment, see Paul Ricoeur, *The Reality of the Historical Past* (Milwaukee, WI: Marquette University Press, 1984): 6–7.

16 Oliver Stone, "On *Nixon* and *JFK*," in Toplin, *Oliver Stone's USA*: 278.

17 Ibid.: 279.

18 In this sequence, Stone's filmmaking is very close to Collingwood's idea that the historian is obliged "to think himself into the action." In Ricoeur, *Reality of the Historical Past*: 7.

19 Oliver Stone, "Stone on Stone's Image," in Toplin, *Oliver Stone's USA*: 53.

20 Hayden White, "The Modernist Event," in Vivan Sobchack, ed., *The Persistence of History: Cinema, Television, and the Modern Event* (New York: Routledge, 1996): 17–38. See also Robert Burgoyne, *Film Nation: Hollywood Looks at U.S. History* (Minneapolis: University of Minnesota Press, 1997): 88–103.

21 Oliver Stone, "On Nixon and JFK," in Toplin, *Oliver Stone's USA*. Stone writes: "The Kennedy murder, which, like Oedipus to the Greeks, has become our national taboo" (p. 297).

22 Oliver Stone, "On *Nixon* and *JFK*," in Toplin, *Oliver Stone's USA*: 284.

23 Robert Rosenstone, "Oliver Stone as Historian," in Toplin, *Oliver Stone's USA*: 8.

CHAPTER 6

THE TOPICAL HISTORICAL FILM: *UNITED 93* AND *WORLD TRADE CENTER*

Simultaneously disruptive and conservative, the narratives of *United 93* and *World Trade Center* occupy an odd netherworld of historical representation – challenging in terms of subject matter, but narrowly circumscribed in their approach. Shaped by the cultural barriers that have been erected around the memory of 9/11, both films are scrupulous in their pursuit of authenticity, and yet focus on such a narrow slice of history that they seem to deflect historical understanding as well as any larger sense of "coming to terms." While not rising to the level of prohibition that surrounded Holocaust representation before *Schindler's List*, the idea that it is still "too soon" to represent 9/11 has permeated much of US culture, a perception that apparently influenced the filmmakers to rigorously delimit their works. As the critic and essayist Frank Rich has commented, however, perhaps it is already "too late"; the event has begun to fade from memory, the culturally therapeutic value of representing the event may no longer hold.[1]

Both *United 93* and *World Trade Center* have been approvingly characterized as politically neutral acts of memorial representation and as straightforward narratives of self-sacrifice and collective determination. Both films perform a certain kind of cultural work, reframing historical trauma as a narrative of heroic agency. Radically different in their visual styles and in the particular elements of the events that they portray, these two subdued and tightly focused works each follow a narrative arc that emphasizes human agency and collective heroic action in the face of overwhelming catastrophe. Sensitive to the demand that representations of 9/11 have a special connection to "discourses of responsibility," the films rehearse a pattern that has emerged as a culturally dominant formula, underscoring the theme of heroism in a much larger landscape of victimization. As in Holocaust and in Hiroshima representations, a kind of reductive legislation of symbolic representation may be taking place. As Adam Lowenstein points out in the context of Hiroshima, the result "is a closing down of the very discussion that might imagine and interpret representation in ways that might answer to the cultural and historical complexity of traumatic events."[2] Nowhere in *United 93* or *World Trade Center* are the compound contexts, the traumatic cultural and social effects, the devastating losses, or the profound alterations of national life that characterize 9/11 registered; instead, linear narrative patterning and classical limitations of character, place and time impose a rigorous and singular structure. The dramatic organization of both works suggests a kind of fixation or obsession, a determined refusal to acknowledge the radical alteration of national life wrought by 9/11.

Rather than observing the discourses of responsibility, limitations of form and content of this sort might be read as a symptom of cultural repression, the "too soon" or "too late" suggesting the skewed temporality of trauma. Understood in terms of the ongoing historical narrative of the United States, 9/11 has begun to seem like a prohibited zone, an event that cannot be assimilated beyond a few singular strands, the isolated bits that confirm a national story of heroism and providential guidance. An unstated consensus seems to be emerging that 9/11 should be considered a hallowed event, that "graven images" should not be made of it, suggesting that just beneath this veneer lurks a sense of fear and dread. The recent refusal of several CBS affiliates to air a documentary on 9/11 at the five-year anniversary, ostensibly because of the strong language used by the firefighters and other rescuers, is a symptom of this tendency, which has become more pronounced over time: the same documentary had been aired twice before on CBS.

In this chapter, I argue that *United 93* and *World Trade Center* function as preliminary attempts to "act out" a historical trauma. In psychoanalysis, a distinction is made between "acting out" and "working through," a distinction that the historian Dominick LaCapra has applied to historical narratives dealing with the Holocaust. Seen as initial dramatic responses to 9/11, the films' insistence on the literal, narrow representation of events can be understood as an example of "acting out," the re-creation of the traumatic event in a form that is largely depleted of context or temporal extension. LaCapra describes "acting out" as a melancholy possession of the subject by the past. "Working through," by contrast, suggests a breaking out; without freeing oneself from trauma, the subject attains a "measure of critical purchase on problems."[3] Despite their emphasis on agency and positive action, *World Trade Center* and *United 93* seem closer to the spirit of melancholy possession than they do to the spirit of attaining a "measure of critical purchase."

Although these works carefully screen out the most catastrophic images and effects of 9/11, they still manifest a disturbing intensity of affect. A sense of adrenalized stasis dominates the tone of each film, a mood compounded by their focus on the profound disconnection, claustrophobia, and sense of helplessness suffered by the characters. Both films emphasize an inability to communicate, numbing isolation, and an almost literal experience of paralysis. Despite the traditional plotting of these works, the traumatic nature of the events of 9/11 is conveyed through their visual and acoustic design. As in melodrama, the tensions in the narrative are in effect somatized, displaced into the body of the film-text.

United 93 presents a powerful dichotomy between the inability to communicate "on the ground" and the surreptitious but effective communication within the plane. A vast network of military aerial surveillance, civilian flight controllers, and government agencies are shown to be unable to sort through conflicting reports, and unable to respond. There is too much information, too many flight plans to consider, too many unknowns in an environment that cannot operate with unknowns. Attempts to understand the timetables, the flight paths, and to coordinate among different civilian and military agencies are shown to be hopelessly ineffective, as overlapping sectors of authority create a further sense of paralysis. The passengers on United Flight 93, on the other hand, are portrayed as effective tacticians, identifying among themselves specific areas of expertise and particular areas of strength. A single-engine pilot among the passengers might be able to land the plane, a former air traffic controller might be able to talk him through it, a black belt in the martial arts will lead the attack on the hijackers. As the film unfolds, the passengers emerge from a condition of atomized inertia to become an effective collective unit dedicated first to survival, and finally to sacrifice. Violence has a face here, and so does agency. As the passengers begin to coordinate their plan of action, their steadiness and concentrated

FIGURE 6.1 The passengers of United 93 move with collective purpose against the terrorist hijackers. *United 93* (2006) [Universal Pictures/Photofest]

determination are set against the increasing agitation of the civilian and military officers and personnel on the ground.

World Trade Center depicts a very different zone of experience, closely focusing on the entrapment of two firefighters in the rubble of the World Trade Center concourse. Here, the depiction is even more circumscribed, almost entirely limited to scenes under the pile, cross-cut with sequences depicting the distress of the families of the two firefighters. In contrast to the nervous, verité visual style of *United 93*, *World Trade Center* maintains a minimalist, nearly abstract visual approach. The scenes under the pile are compositions in black, gray, and white, as if they were drawings in charcoal. The static aspect of these scenes – both men are pinned down and unable to move – at times seems like something out of the avant-garde plays of Samuel Beckett, where forms of emptiness, nothingness, and the utter absence of event express the profound isolation of the characters. Here, in long sequences underground, we see only the lips of the characters moving, scenes that are extended to the point of discomfort on the part of the viewer. In contrast, the extraordinarily bright and vivid portrayals of their two wives, anxiously awaiting some kind of reliable information about their husbands, and the even more day-glo dreams of the two firefighters, are like being plunged into a painting by Van Gogh, unfathomably beautiful and colored so intensely that they seem enameled.

E. Ann Kaplan and Ban Wang describe cinematic attempts to render historical trauma as a somewhat paradoxical endeavor. Trauma, they point out, is often considered the ultimate limit of representation, the collapse of symbolic systems, what is left after the destruction of the capacity to signify. "The traumatic experience has affect only, not meaning . . . the affect is too much to be registered cognitively in the brain."[4] In these definitions, the traumatic event is so profoundly disturbing to the victim that it cannot be communicated; its symptoms emerge only in the form of nightmares, hallucinations, incoherent speech, or phobias. When applied to wide-scale historical events, however, this type of clinical description, based as it is on individual cases, short-circuits both historical analysis and narrative representation. Although many cultural critics have adopted this asymbolic model based on individual, clinical cases, it clearly falls short of providing a discursive paradigm for dealing with many of the historical events of the twentieth and twenty-first centuries, which have increasingly consisted of overwhelmingly catastrophic occurrences, what many critics and some historians have called traumatic historical events. Recent history is more and more a series of shocks on an unprecedented scale, events that confound existing forms of historical explanation, and that require a new representational vocabulary.

Calling for a revision of the asymbolic clinical model, Kaplan and Wang make the striking point that "history has shown that intensely traumatic events have spawned more narratives and images, rather than less."[5] They write that the history of modernity, the history of the twentieth and twenty-first centuries, has in fact consisted of a series of cultural shocks and traumatic events. In fact, many early theorists of modernity, such as Walter Benjamin and George Simmel, were already writing in the 1920s and 1930s on the traumatic effects of modern life. And contemporary theorists, such as Hayden White and Thomas Elsaesser, have written extensively about the obsessive, traumatic nature of twentieth- and twenty-first-century historical events. Central to this analysis is the fact that the extreme, compound nature of "modernist" events is reinforced by the media: continuous video replays, the endlessly repeating loops of disasters such as the collapse of the World Trade Center, the obsessive coverage of the Katrina storm and flood, and the space shuttle disasters speak not to the collapse of signifying capacity but rather to the deep connection between saturation media coverage and cultural trauma. The attack on the World Trade Center, as one critic has said, was "the most widely observed breaking news event in human history, seen that day in still photos, on the internet, or on television by an estimated two billion people, nearly a third of the human race."[6]

Reviewing Freud's various writings on trauma, Kaplan and Wang also take issue with the traditional clinical reading of trauma. For Freud, trauma is not the cleavage that neuroscience refers to, but rather a "delay in attention to the event," and a subsequent process of revision of memories assisted by fantasy. For studies of cultural and historical traumatic memories, what is important here is the temporary "forgetting" that Freud finds characteristic of traumatic memory, followed by a period of revision. Kaplan writes that "cultures too can split off what cannot be dealt with at a specific historical moment." As traumatic memories begin "leaking out" into cultural forms, however, narratives and images become critical indexes, modes of both "acting out" and "working through." La Capra describes the phase of "acting out" as the "melancholy possession of the subject by the repressed past."[7] "Working through," by contrast, is an attempt at breakout, offering a "degree of critical purchase." As Kaplan and Wang write, the visual media have become a cultural institution in which the traumatic experience of modernity can be "recognized, negotiated, and reconfigured."[8]

The impact of 9/11 on national identity has been a source of controversy and debate among historians. While the political consequences of the attacks have been prominently considered in public discourse, the deeper questions of national self-definition have been only slowly working their way to the surface. For some historians, 9/11 precipitated a dramatic reframing of the narrative of nation, provoking a belated recognition of US history in relation to the rest of the world. Understanding American history in terms of global and intersecting lines of power, domination, and resistance, some historians now view the American Revolution, for example, from a transnational perspective, as a small part of a story of global competition among empires such as England, Spain, and France. Implicated in global struggles from the colonial period, the United States can be seen in terms of a nexus of global interests, both positive and negative, an identity that was suddenly brought into bold relief by 9/11. As one writer says, "American history is being studied less as the story of a neatly packaged nation state and more in a global context, as part of something much larger."[9]

Such a focus changes the look of American history; in these approaches, the traditional emphasis on the Cold War during the 1950s and 1960s has begun to give way in importance to postcolonial and neocolonial frameworks. And the history of ethnic migrations, and in particular, the history of Muslims in America, has begun to displace the traditional focus on superpower politics. 9/11 also brought into relief a very different tendency in American political and historical thought, one characterized by a focus on the doctrine of exceptionalism. A doctrine that had been largely discredited by the rise of social histories in the last decade, American exceptionalism has returned as a powerful paradigm among neoconservatives. In this view, the United States is understood to be unique among nations, a viewpoint that emphasizes the special role America plays in the world, "what makes it different from others." In this understanding, the underlying ethical vision of the American story, its central theme, is made visible by its opposition to competing large-scale ideologies. The value of the civilization represented by the United States has, since 9/11, become increasingly clear to those who hold to the exceptionalist viewpoint. In particular, contemporary struggles against Islamic fundamentalism have been compared to the struggle against fascism and the Cold War, a framing of the event that has become increasingly prominent in conservative discourse. As one historian writes, "the massive conflict with fascism and then the cold war focused attention on what is our civilization, why is it different from others. With that came a certain sense of heightened attachment to our civilization and a desire to defend and protect it."[10]

Both of these perspectives address a topical event, a discrete occurrence – the attacks of 9/11 – as decisive alterations of the narrative of nation. In these views, the nation's identity has been marked indelibly by a single set of events, a change that extends to the national past. Reconsidering the past from the perspective of the present, historians have drawn widely divergent conclusions about the patterns that the event illuminates, as if they were looking at the past through different color filters. Both perspectives, however, have one important theme in common: they both assume that existing historical frameworks are more or less adequate to situate and express the events of 9/11 in a larger worldview. In these accounts, the experience of catastrophe can be integrated into a larger pattern, become meaningful in terms of historical viewpoint, and can be represented in a framework guided by a sense of the connectedness of events, their causal linkages, their continuity with an existing cultural narrative, whether it be that of postcolonial studies or of American exceptionalism.

The traumatic nature of contemporary historical events remains unaddressed in both accounts. A very different "take" on the experience of the World Trade Center disaster, in particular, comes from Slavoj Žižek, who writes of the twentieth century's passion for the Real:

> In contrast to the nineteenth-century of utopian or "scientific" projects and ideals, plans for the future, the twentieth century aimed at delivering the thing itself . . . The ultimate and defining moment of the twentieth century was the direct experience of the Real as opposed to everyday social reality – the Real in its extreme violence as the price to be paid for peeling off the deceptive layers of reality. . . . We can perceive the collapse of the WTC towers as the climactic conclusion of twentieth-century art's 'passion for the Real' – the "terrorists" themselves did not do it primarily to provoke real material damage, but *for the spectacular effect of it* . . . we were all forced to experience what the 'compulsion to repeat' and *jouissance* beyond the pleasure principle are: we wanted to see it again and again, the same shots were repeated *ad nauseam*, and the uncanny satisfaction we got from it was *jouissance* at its purest. . . . The question we should have asked ourselves as we stared at the TV screens on September 11 is simply: *where have we already seen the same thing over and over again?*[11]

Žižek's provocative assertions convey a powerful sense of the enabling relationship between trauma and contemporary media forms. Genocidal wars, invasions, catastrophic attacks, and natural disasters are magnified by the visual media. The vivid kinesthetic experience of the cinema, in particular, has been linked to an experience of "vicarious traumatization," as Kaplan puts it.

The stylistic feature of *United 93* that has received the most critical attention is the handheld camera, which conveys an extraordinary quality of immediacy and urgency. As the film progresses, the camerawork becomes increasingly jagged, with the speed and intensity of movement, the fragmentary split-second images, and the whip pans of the camera creating a tachycardic rhythm that pummels the audience. In the opening shots of the film however, a stately and smooth rhythm dominates, as the film provides still shots of the hijackers as they pray in the predawn light, beautiful helicopter shots of New York, and long, stationary shots of mundane details such as the fueling of the airplane. The steady increase in speed and rhythm is all the more effective for its gradual introduction.

The other major stylistic trope of *United 93* is its powerful use of parallel editing. Cutting among the interiors of the plane, the National Air Traffic Control Center in Herndon, Virginia, air traffic control in New York, Boston, Cleveland, and the Northeast Air Defense Sector, the film presents a powerful study of what Eisenstein might call poly-phonic montage, the simultaneous advance of multiple strands of the story, orchestrated in the form of controlled and graduated shocks to the audience. Early in his theater career, Eisenstein advocated placing firecrackers under the seats of the audience; later, he refined the tech-nique of shocking and moving the audience through the orchestration of color, music, rhythm, and lighting. In *United 93*, the intercutting is full of contrasting visual tones, the red gloom of the control tower in Boston, the green hue of the control room at NEADS, the soft white of the National Air Traffic Control Center, the wide windows of the New York control tower looking across the water onto the smoking towers, and the white fluorescence of the interior of the plane itself. The technique of parallel editing here renders in a detailed way activ-ities in six different locations, each of which is distinctively colored and clearly defined. The six locations depict a world of interiors, a high-tech universe dedicated to rational understanding, assessment, and control. Paul Greengrass, the film's director, calls air traffic control a "beautifully calibrated machine . . . our modern life is essentially about systems." Indeed, the word "control" figures in the name of nearly all of the spaces the film depicts, with the exception of the aircraft itself. Each of these "control" spaces is plunged into near-panic as the morning advances and reports of hijacked planes keep coming in, a total of 29 reported hijackings in the course of the day. As the film progresses, the use of long shots and even medium shots diminish: cross-cutting is reduced to close-ups of one location cut directly into close-ups from another location, heighten-ing the tension.

Benedict Anderson has linked the concept of modern national life to a particular sense of space and time, in particular, to a sense of simultaneity and parallelism. This is expressed most clearly, for Anderson, in the forms of the realist novel and the daily newspaper, both of which convey a sense of temporal coincidence and simultaneity, both of which suggest a multitude of unrelated actions occurring in a single community. What Walter Benjamin calls "homogeneous, empty time" is directly related to the image of the modern nation: in Anderson's words, "the idea of a sociological organism moving calendrically through homogeneous, empty time is a precise analogue of the nation, which is also conceived as a solid community moving steadily up (or down) in history." The temporality of the novel and the newspaper, the impression they create of parallel lives moving along parallel pathways, "allowed people to imagine the special community that is the nation," forming what he calls a "complex gloss upon the word 'meanwhile.' "[12]

FIGURE 6.2 The Northeast Air Defense Sector, with its old-fashioned "green-eyes" radar screens, tries valiantly to cope with the 9/11 crisis. *United 93* (2006) [Universal Pictures/Photofest]

United 93 presents a striking rehearsal – and rupture – of this theme. The simultaneity and parallelism driving the narrative, set in bold relief in the portrait of the various air traffic control centers, creates a snapshot of the nation as it moves, minute by minute, not into "homogeneous, empty time," but into a national crisis. The opening scenes of the film underline the ordinary, daily aspects of American life – the lines at the airport, the gathering and waiting in the terminal and on the aircraft itself, the beginnings of a new workday at the different control centers. Into this collective zone of homogeneous empty time, in which efficiency, administrative control, planning, and "service" are paramount, explodes the very different temporality of the terrorists. Systematically organized toward an endpoint of destruction and death, the hijackers' narrative is structured around a single moment, a vanishing point, realized in the moment of impact. Shattering the insulated daily course of national life, the eruption of terror ruptures the parallelism and continuity of ordinary life, as the radical destructive and aggressive culture of the terrorists reintroduces "absolute negativity" into the administered world of goods and services, pulling the parallelism and simultaneity of the modern nation, so clearly delineated in the early scenes of the film, into a zone

FIGURE 6.3 Ben Sliney, head of the National Air Traffic Control Center, playing himself during the 9/11 crisis. *United 93* (2006) [Universal Pictures/Photofest]

of incomprehension and panicked anxiety, into a zone that might best be described as traumatic.[13]

Žižek compares the planes hitting the towers, particularly the second plane, recorded for all time and flying with wings seemingly outstretched for the camera, to the famous scene in Hitchcock's *The Birds*, when Melanie, flush with flirtatious triumph, is suddenly, incomprehensibly, attacked by a gull as she traverses Bodega Bay. The gull enters our perspective as a blot, unseen and unnoticed by Melanie, who is attacked in the middle of a brilliant, cloudless day. *World Trade Center* begins with a similar expression of daily life governed by a sense of parallelism and order, of an idyllic New York morning. The morning routines of the two main characters are sketched in what narrative theory calls the frequentative mode, a description of daily events as they unfold in a customary way, a single description standing for a whole series.

World Trade Center can be characterized as a work of commemoration. As such, it stands somewhere between the discourses of traumatic memory, of history as fragments of unnarratable ruin, and the activity of rememoration that the French historian Pierre Nora calls *lieux*

FIGURE 6.4 Officer Will Jimeno (Michael Pena) notices the shadow of one of the planes, a blot that enters the frame. *World Trade Center* (2006) [Universal Pictures/Photofest]

de mémoire, or "places of memory."[14] The film conveys both the loss of coherence, the profound atomization and isolation associated with an incomprehensible event, as well as the impulse to salvage and record the memory of the occurrence. Although the repetition, the acting out, and the numbing amnesia that accompany cultural trauma would seem to be radically opposed to the discourses of memory that Nora identifies as a central preoccupation of modern life, with its commemorations, heritage movements, and salvage operations, both of these responses speak to a sense of loss and alienation from the past, and to some extent, a sense of panic.

Nora's argument concerning the role of memory in contemporary life revolves around the principle of reenactment. Because our relationship to the historical past is fractured and discontinuous – a consequence of modern industrial and postindustrial life with its wrenching changes and discontinuities from one generation to another – Nora argues that we are now engaged "in a paradoxical search for proximity"; we seek the continuity of the present with the past through places of memory, reenactments, and objects that function as repositories of past experiences. Memory projects, witness testimonies, oral histories, museums of daily life, and so on, are now ubiquitous, a symptom of our fear of forgetting because of our actual condition of disconnection from the past. He refers to the current hypertrophy of memory as "hallucinatory re-creations of the past," provoked by our desire to experience what has forever disappeared: "Memory situates remembrance in a sacred context . . . Memory wells up from groups that it welds together . . . Memory is rooted in the concrete, in space, gesture, image, and object."[15]

At first glance Nora's description of the cultural turn toward memory, with its nostalgia, its idealization, and its powerful role in forging social bonds would seem far removed from the discourses surrounding 9/11. The perspective described by Žižek as compulsive repetition and vicarious traumatization would seem to be radically opposed to the impulse conveyed by the regimes of memory Nora describes. As Žižek writes, "when, days after September 11, 2001, our gaze was transfixed by the images of the plane hitting one of the WTC towers, we were all forced to experience what the 'compulsion to repeat' and *jouissance* beyond the pleasure principle are: we wanted to see it again and again."[16] However, *World Trade Center* also calls to mind the commemorative activity associated with the places of memory, a desire, as Pierre Nora describes it, to "stop time, to inhibit forgetting, to fix a state of things, to immortalize death, and to materialize the immaterial."[17] Enacted in what is perhaps the most politically and socially charged "place of memory" in the world – the zone now known as Ground Zero – *World Trade Center*, with its twin pulls toward the void and towards the forging of a social compact, registers both trauma and commemoration; the film can be read as both symptom and as hallucinatory re-creation designed to "stop time" and "inhibit forgetting."

The first image of *World Trade Center* is a digital clock on the bedstand of Sergeant McLoughlin, set to the obscenely early hour of 3:29 A.M. As the opening of the film unfolds, we see the five main police officers who will figure in the story making their way into the morning workday, moving along separate pathways into the city. Here, the twin towers are first seen, initially from the George Washington Bridge against the "dawn's early light," and then from New Jersey, from Staten Island, from uptown Manhattan, viewed in closer and closer shots from all the radial points of the city. The film's opening has something of a "city film" aspect, reminiscent of Ruttman's *Berlin: Symphony of a Great City* or Vertov's *Man with a Movie Camera*. The predawn transportation, by car, by train, and by ferry, the early morning labor of the workers in the meatpacking district, the daily routines of morning dogwalkers, and above all, the catalogue of familiar New York sites, the Empire State Building, the Chrysler Building, and the Statue of Liberty, are

FIGURE 6.5 The ruins of the World Trade Center, a "place of memory" fraught with emotion. *World Trade Center* (2006) [Universal Pictures/Photofest]

rendered from ground level or sea level. Like Vertov and Ruttman, Oliver Stone draws a familiar portrait of the city, picturing it as a place that is both prosaic and beautiful – and the epitome of a particular historical moment.

The catastrophe that follows is rendered in a very different mode, however, almost surrealistically, as in Lautréamont's description of poetry as the "chance encounter of an umbrella and a sewing machine on a dissecting table." In 1918, Louis Aragon celebrated modern life and the power of cinema to evoke fascination, focusing especially on the power of "really common objects" such as corned beef and tins of polish, a newspaper or a packet of cigarettes: "Those letters advertising a make of soap are the equivalent of characters on an obelisk or the inscriptions in a book of spells: they describe the fate of an era."[18] These ideas have never seemed more pertinent: *World Trade Center* evokes the strange silence, the "magnification of objects" that the Surrealists prized. In this regard, it is the opposite of *United 93*, with its statically charged radio transmissions, its urgent exchanges, and its mood of panic. In *World Trade Center*, when the Port Authority Police Department personnel arrive at the twin towers, they appear stunned by the rain of white paper from countless office files, by the almost slow-motion transit of ashen-faced

FIGURE 6.6 Sergeant McCloughlin (Nicolas Cage) with his team of volunteers, about to cross a historical threshold. *World Trade Center* (2006) [Universal Pictures/Photofest]

office workers away from the site, and by the sight of a single, fallen businessman. And as the rescue workers pass through the doomed retail arcades of Tower 1, the shop-window signs advertising Victoria's Secret, J. Crew, Johnston and Murphy, and Express seem to describe "the fate of an era." In the words of Aragon, "On the screen, objects that were a few moments ago sticks of furniture or books of cloakroom tickets are transformed to the point where they take on menacing or enigmatic meanings."[19]

The entombment of the two main characters that follows narrows the focus radically. Alternating among lengthy sequences in the dark with the two surviving characters and the extraordinarily vivid portrayals of the characters' wives and families as they try to cope with the absence of concrete information, the film becomes at times a kind of dream script, almost as if Stone were reprising, in a more anxious key, the strangely discomforting Norman Rockwell-style opening montage of *Born on the Fourth of July*. The two main characters, communicating in their imaginations with their wives, and in the case of Jimeno, with Jesus, are lit and presented as spectacularly beautiful dream images and memories. Verging on the maudlin, these dream scenes turn into lengthy real-life sequences, with the memories and imaginings of the two trapped characters serving as the conduit to full-length scenes of their wives and families as they try to cope. Although these above-ground sequences are ordinary in every way, depicting the tensions and anxieties of domestic life under extreme pressure, they retain a vividness of imagination and imagery that lifts them above the prosaic. To continue with the surrealist metaphor, the film here presents a kind of "synthetic critique" of daily life. When Donna in her Jersey home must step around the big hole in the flooring of her "new kitchen," yet to be finished by McCloughlin; when Alison walks out into her New Jersey neighborhood at night to see the intermittent blue light of all the television sets in every little bungalow flaring and illuminating the block, some attuned to the tragedy unfolding and some not; and when the congregations of the lost are seen gathered together in the hospital waiting room, the film succeeds in defamiliarizing the everyday. A stop light that won't turn, a trip to the well-stocked drugstore, a deserted street: these become the raw materials of a twenty-first-century wasteland, with the love song of Prufrock thrown in.

As works of commemoration dedicated to the close rendering of two moments of positive agency, *World Trade Center* and *United 93* pull in two different directions. Each comes to a strikingly different resolution. *United 93* concludes with a sudden blackout and silence as the plane crashes to the ground, despite the powerful catharsis of the passengers overcoming the hijackers and rushing the cockpit. The sudden, devastating end of the film might be compared to the endings of World War I films. As Pierre Sorlin writes about films set during World War I, they typically end with a vision of complete devastation, delivered without comment by the filmmakers: "the emptiness of the end overwhelms the spectator: makes them feel as if they have been caught up in some vast, impersonal, meaningless disaster . . . no one has been spared. It is like a world's end: no story can be told, there is not the possibility even of a history."[20] *World Trade Center*, by contrast, ends with McCloughlin emerging into light, and with a powerful sense of renewal and reunion.

This difference suggests that the films serve different cultural needs. *World Trade Center* builds on the symbolic aura associated with the specific site of the attacks, the Ground Zero location which has been re-created in the film to breathtaking effect. As Nora characterizes it, the places of memory must be endowed with a "symbolic aura" that resonates in the public imagination. Memory, as he puts it, clings to places just as history clings to events. In its concentrated attention to place rather than event, the film focuses on a specific site, the symbolic center where the memory of 9/11 is concentrated. *World Trade Center* expresses the

FIGURE 6.7 The love song of memory: Donna McCloughlin (Maria Bello) as John remembers her. *World Trade Center* (2006) [Universal Pictures/Photofest]

audience's emotional relationship to place, condensed in the ruins of ground zero, and extending outwards to Trinity Church and to the streets and neighborhoods adjacent to the site. It reenacts the past in terms of place, instantiating Pierre Nora's description of the "places of memory."

The symbolic aura connected with place typically draws on the symbolism of death and rebirth, evident in the popularity of battlefields, for example, or the Vietnam Memorial, or other places of pilgrimage. In *World Trade Center*, the theme of rebirth is asserted amid the ruins of the towers, and is conveyed principally by the images of the two women whose stories alternate with the two trapped and immobilized protagonists. When McCloughlin is lifted, finally, from the bowels of the ruined Trade Center into the light, he is hallucinating, imagining himself having a close-up conversation, a reunion, with his wife, Donna. The history that the film presents is folded into memory, and recoded as a love story, a double love story, a point that Oliver Stone acknowledges on the commentary track.

The film creates a metaphoric connection between acts of individual memory, so positively celebrated here, and the collective memory of 9/11. Memory, of course, is a singular, individual experience, connected to the deepest sense of one's self. St. Augustine crafted a striking metaphor:

FIGURE 6.8 The future, the past, and the memory that links them. Will Jimeno (Michael Pena) and his wife Allison (Maggie Gyllenhaal) discuss the name of their unborn child. *World Trade Center* (2006) [Universal Pictures/Photofest]

referring to the "vast palaces of memory," he writes of the interior life as "Memory's huge cavern, with its mysterious, secret, and indescribable nooks and crannies."[21] In *World Trade Center*, the activity of memory becomes literalized, projected onto the "nooks and crannies" of the ruin by McCloughlin and Jimeno, and thus projected onto the screen of contemporary culture in the collective experience of the cinema. The film creates a kind of affective community of memory, a sense of solidarity with the trapped victims. By celebrating individual memory of the most intimate kind in the context of the World Trade Center attacks, the film reworks the traumatic cultural memory of 9/11, with it collapsing towers and explosions of smoke and debris, into a form that clearly gestures toward the process of "working through."

United 93 conveys a very different message. Rigorously focused on the real-time unfolding of the events, there are no escapes into memory. The film, as Greengrass says, is focused on the present and on the future: "we are all on United 93 . . . This is where we are today . . . [these are] images of that day, but also images of our tomorrow." Conceived as a call to vigilance and action, *United 93* ends with a shot of two sets of hands wrestling for control of the airplane, "a fight for the controls of our world." Where the most expressive images of *World Trade Center* are the close-ups of faces, in the blackness of the rubble or in the dreamy beauty of the memory scenes, the iconic shots in *United 93* are the close-ups of hands. The praying hands of the hijackers before they begin their day, the expressive gestures of the passengers as they plan their attack and make their last phone calls, the outstretched, bloodied hands of the terrorist co-pilot as he prays for the last time – the concentrated attention on hands in the scenes on the plane convey a powerful set of messages. Both the hijackers and the passengers are defined by their hands, in both concrete and metaphorical ways. They are agents of the narrative, and of the historical event.

"National crisis" are the last words heard from the ground, as Sliney, the national air traffic control director, shuts down and grounds all flights in the United States and entering from other countries. The scenes that follow are limited to the struggle on board the flight, which is rendered as an extraordinary melee, in which adrenaline and dread are equally mixed. The sudden blackout at the end of the film is softened only by the continuation of the orchestral score for a few moments, a single electronic chord. The ending of the film thus matches the opening, which began in darkness with the sound of one of the hijackers praying.

United 93 provides a possible example of what E. Ann Kaplan and Joshua Hirsch have called "vicarious traumatization." Hirsch describes this effect through reference to Nietzsche: "If something is to stay in the memory it must be burned in: only that which never ceases to *hurt* stays in the memory."[22] While Hirsch's work concerns Holocaust documentaries such as *The Death Camps* (1945), *Mein Kampf* (1960), and *Night and Fog* (1955), and is, he writes, hypothetical, the concept of vicarious trauma experienced through film provides a way of opening up the discourse of the historical film in an interesting direction. What is historically thinkable, he writes, "is partly constituted by the conventions of the historical film genre . . . a cinematic discourse of trauma . . . [upsets] the spectator's expectations not only of history in general, but also of the historical film in particular."[23] The project of representing traumatic historical experience in film has emerged forcefully in a variety of contexts, beginning with World War I and continuing into the present. In the postwar period, films that have been discussed as examples of traumatic historical representation are chiefly documentaries, European art films such as *Hiroshima, Mon Amour* (1959), or American experimental film and video, such as works on Abu Ghraib, Iraq, and 9/11. *United 93* employs the modernist discourse of traumatic representation, with a documentary visual style, an emphasis on "real time," and a discontinuous editing technique, within a general, mainstream narrative form, featuring a unified, compressed storyline that distills the events of 9/11 into a single dramatic narrative. Rather than working to "explode" the conventions of the historical film, *United 93* draws them into a single, almost unbearably concentrated expression. The sense of entrapment, the accelerated and chaotic camera movements, the jagged cutting, all contribute to an extraordinary sense of realism that aims for something different: to break down the protective defenses of the audience in order to register a traumatic historical event that is not of the past, but exists in the present and the future. As Greengrass says in his commentary track: "this is where we are today."

From this perspective, *World Trade Center* and *United 93* seem to define starkly different approaches to representing the historical event of 9/11. *World Trade Center* draws on the discourses of commemoration. However, in its defamiliarization of daily life, its surrealistic juxtapositions, and in its palpable sense of loss and missed connections, an essential melancholy comes through. The past "possesses" the film despite its attempt to stop time and inhibit forgetting. *United 93*, by contrast, attempts to break down the defenses of the audience in order to prevent the traumatic events of 9/11 from being relegated to memory. As Cathy Caruth has written, it functions like "a voice that cries out from the wound."[24]

Alison Landsberg has coined the striking term "prosthetic memory" to describe the way mass cultural technologies enable individuals to experience, as if they were memories, events that were witnessed only second-hand. The modes of experience, sensation, and history that are made available through mass technology provide vivid experiences of the past that can shape subjectivity. In a way that at first seems strikingly similar to the concept of "vicarious traumatization," Landsberg defines prosthetic memory as "memories that circulate publicly, that are not organically based, but that are nonetheless experienced with one's own body." Prosthetic memories, she claims, especially those created by the cinema, "become part of one's own personal archive of experience." Prosthetic memories enable a sensuous engagement with past lives and past experiences, and can serve as "the basis for mediated collective identification."[25]

The role of historical film in conveying and reenacting traumatic events can be understood in both positive and negative terms. Landsberg's concept of prosthetic memory describes the positive slope of this experience: cinema enables memories and experiences to be shared in a muted version of the event itself; "the 'remembering' of particularly traumatic events of the collective past inevitably affects both the identity of the individual person and his or her previously accepted worldview . . .

'strategic remembering' . . . has the power, then, to support a sense of collective social responsibility.'[26] The extraordinary care taken by both Stone and Greengrass to make the portrayal of events as accurate as possible, to the point of mixing together real-life participants and actors in both films, speaks to the impulse to create an interface with past lives and past bodies. The prospect of forging a new sense of collective social responsibility is an explicit part of the message of both *World Trade Center* and *United 93* both of which, in their own way, ask the question: "What do we do now?"

On the other hand, the cinema can relay images of the past in a way that may have a secondary traumatizing effect, or worse, come to assume a numbing familiarity. Or even worse yet, become a stage setting for political manipulation, the aestheticization of history that Walter Benjamin warned about in 1935, culminating in his argument that war has become a form of artistic gratification for a sense perception changed by technology: "[mankind's] self-alienation has reached such a degree that it can experience its own destruction as an aesthetic pleasure of the first order."[27]

The question I have been pursuing throughout this chapter is the role of film in articulating the shift in historical consciousness that 9/11 has produced. Both films insist that 9/11 marks a fundamental dividing point. As evidenced by these two films, the initial aesthetic response is a repurposed realism – a highly valorized sense of the integrity of space and character, reminiscent of early neo-realism, combined with unpredictable editing rhythms, disconcerting pacing, and an expressionist color palette. Will this be sufficient, however, to avoid the fate that Frank Rich predicts for these films, that they will soon come to seem escapist in comparison with contemporary geopolitical reality? The traumatic historical film, as represented by *United 93* and *World Trade Center*, provides a limited but useful sense of the power of visual representations to preserve the memory of traumatic events. Whether films and other modes of visual media can also contribute to a "working through" of traumatic historical experience remains an open question.

Notes

1 Frank Rich, "Too Soon? It's Too Late for 'United 93,'" *New York Times*, May 7, 2006.

2 Adam Lowenstein, "Allegorizing Hiroshima: Shindo Kaneto's *Onibaba* as Trauma Text," in E. Ann Kaplan and Ban Wang, eds., *Trauma and Cinema: Cross-Cultural Explorations* (Hong Kong University Press, 2004): 147.

3   Dominick LaCapra, *Representing the Holocaust* (Ithaca, NY: Cornell University Press, 1994): 209.

4   E. Ann Kaplan and Ban Wang, "Introduction: From Traumatic Paralysis to the Force Field of Modernity," in Kaplan and Wang, *Trauma and Cinema*: 5.

5   Ibid.: 12.

6   David Friend, "The Man in the Window," *Vanity Fair*, September 2006: 286.

7   LaCapra's description is here set forth by Kaplan and Wang, *Trauma and Cinema*: 6.

8   Ibid.: 17.

9   Janny Scott, "9/11 Leaves Its Mark on History Classes," *New York Times*, September 6, 2006.

10 Stephan Thernstrom, quoted in ibid.

11 Slavoj Žižek, *Welcome to the Desert of the Real!* (London and New York: Verso, 2002): 5–6, 12, 17.

12 Benedict Anderson, *Imagined Communities: Reflections on the Origin and Spread of Nationalism* (London: Verso, 1991): 25.

13 Žižek, *Welcome to the Desert of the Real*: 142.

14 Pierre Nora, *Realms of Memory: Conflict and Division*, Vol. 1, trans. Arthur Goldhammer (New York: Columbia University Press, 1996).

15 Quoted in William Guynn, *Writing History in Film* (New York and London: Routledge, 2006): 175.

16 Žižek, *Welcome to the Desert of the Real!*: 11–12.

17 Pierre Nora, quoted in Guynn, *Writing History in Film*: 176.

18 See Louis Aragon, "On Décor," in Paul Hammond, ed., *The Shadow and Its Shadow: Surrealist Writings on the Cinema* (London: BFI Publications, 1978): 29–31.

19 Ibid.: 29.

20 Pierre Sorlin, "Cinema and the Memory of the Great War," in Michael Paris, ed., *The First World War and Popular Cinema* (New Brunswick, NJ: Rutgers University Press, 2000).

21 Guynn, *Writing History in Film*: 169.

22 Joshua Hirsch, "Post-Traumatic Cinema and the Holocaust Documentary," in Kaplan and Wang, *Trauma and Cinema*: 93–121.

23 Ibid.: 102.

24 Cathy Caruth, *Unclaimed Experience: Trauma, Narrative, and History* (Baltimore. MD: Johns Hopkins University Press, 1996): 2.

25 Alison Landsberg, *Prosthetic Memory* (New York: Columbia University Press, 2004).

26 Ibid.: 152.

27 Walter Benjamin, "The Work of Art in the Age of Mechanical Reproduction," in *Illuminations*, trans. Harry Zohn (New York: Schocken Books, 1969): 242.

INDEX

CPSIA information can be obtained
at www.ICGtesting.com
Printed in the USA
BVHW04s0555260818
525235BV00042B/375/P